T0318618

Africa and the Challenges of the Twenty-first Century

This publication is a product of CODESRIA's 13th General Assembly

Africa and the Challenges of the Twenty-first Century

Keynote Addresses delivered at
the 13th General Assembly of CODESRIA
(Rabat, Morocco, December 2011)

Edited by
Ebrima Sall

CODESRIA

Council for the Development of Social Science Research in Africa
DAKAR

CODESRIA
Avenue Cheikh Anta Diop, Angle Canal IV
BP 3304 Dakar, 18524, Senegal
Website: www.codesria.org

ISBN: 978-2-86978-601-1

Typesetter: Sériane Camara Ajavon
Cover Designer: Ibrahima Fofana

Distributed in Africa by CODESRIA
Distributed elsewhere by African Books Collective, Oxford, UK.
Website: www.africanbookscollective.com

The Council for the Development of Social Science Research in Africa (CODESRIA) is an independent organisation whose principal objectives are to facilitate research, promote research-based publishing and create multiple forums geared towards the exchange of views and information among African researchers. All these are aimed at reducing the fragmentation of research in the continent through the creation of thematic research networks that cut across linguistic and regional boundaries.

CODESRIA publishes *Africa Development*, the longest standing Africa based social science journal; *Afrika Zamani*, a journal of history; the *African Sociological Review*, the *African Journal of International Affairs*; *Africa Review of Books* and the *Journal of Higher Education in Africa*. The Council also co-publishes the *Africa Media Review*; *Identity, Culture and Politics: An Afro-Asian Dialogue*; *The African Anthropologist* and the *Afro-Arab Selections for Social Sciences*. The results of its research and other activities are also disseminated through its Working Paper Series, Green Book Series, Monograph Series, Book Series, Policy Briefs and the CODESRIA Bulletin. Select CODESRIA publications are also accessible online at www.codesria.org.

CODESRIA would like to express its gratitude to the Swedish International Development Cooperation Agency (SIDA), the International Development Research Centre (IDRC), the Ford Foundation, the Carnegie Corporation of New York (CCNY), the Norwegian Agency for Development Cooperation (NORAD), the Danish Agency for International Development (DANIDA), the Netherlands Ministry of Foreign Affairs, the Rockefeller Foundation, the Open Society Foundations (OSFs), TrustAfrica, UNESCO, UN Women, the African Capacity Building Foundation (ACBF) and the Government of Senegal for supporting its research, training and publication programmes.

Contents

Contributors

Ifi Amadiume is a Nigerian scholar, poet, ethnographer and essayist; she is also a member of CODESRIA's Scientific Committee. She had her early education in Nigeria before moving to Britain in 1971. An outstanding scholar, she is a Professor of Religion and African American Studies Program at Dartmouth College. A tenured full professor since 1999, she has also been Chair of the African and African American Studies Program at Dartmouth College. She has a double BA (Honors 1978) degree in an African language (Hausa) and Social Anthropology from the School of Oriental and African Studies, and a University of London PhD in Social Anthropology (1983). She has researched and taught in African Studies in Nigeria, Britain and the United States of America. Her work has made a tremendous contribution to new ways of thinking of sex and gender, the question of power and women's contributions to history and culture.

Souleymane Bachir Diagne is a Senegalese philosopher. He obtained his PhD from Université Paris I La Sorbonne, France, with a dissertation entitled "Philosophie symbolique et algèbre de logique" (Symbolic Philosophy and Logical Algebra). He has taught in many universities, including Université Cheikh Anta Diop, Dakar, Senegal and Northwestern Evanston University, USA. He currently teaches at Columbia University, USA.

Bachir Diagne is a co-director of Ethiopiques, a Senegalese journal on literature and philosophy. He is a member of the editorial board of many prestigious journals. These include the *Revue d'histoire des mathématiques* which is published by the Société des mathématiques de France, and *Présence africaine* and *Diogenes* published by UNESCO's International Council of Philosophy and Social Sciences. He was once the President of CODESRIA's Scientific Committee, and still remains an active member of the institution. He has also been a member of the Comité africain et malgache pour l'enseignement supérieur (CAMES) and UNESCO's Conseil du Futur.

In 2005, Souleymane Bachir Diagne was named as one of the twenty-five greatest thinkers of the world by *Le Nouvel Observateur* (Paris).

Professor Diagne has numerous publications to his credit in the fields of the history of logics and philosophy, especially in Africa and the Islamic world. He was greatly inspired by Gaston Berger and this has resulted in two of his publications – *Gaston Berger: Introduction à la philosophie de l'avenir* (1997) and

Reconstruire le sens. Textes et enjeux de prospectives africaines (2001). His current research interests are focused on modern challenges such as: identity and belonging, The universe and pluralism, God, modernity and traditions. By recently revisiting the thoughts of Muhammad Iqbal, Leopold Sedar Senghor, Henri Bergson and Kwasi Wiredu, Souleymane Bachir Diagne underlines the necessity of intellectual thinking which allows us to go beyond exclusion and intolerance to build a society that is more open. This is well articulated in his two recent publications: *Islam and Open Society, Fidelity and Movement in the Philosophy of Muhammad Iqbal* (2010), *African Art as Philosophy: Senghor, Bergson and the Idea of Negritude* (2011).

Jayati Ghosh was born in 1955. She was educated at Delhi University, Jawaharlal Nehru University (JNU) and the University of Cambridge. She got her PhD in 1984 from Cambridge University. Her doctoral thesis was entitled "Non Capitalist Land Rent: Theories and the Case of North India". She is now Professor of Economics at the Centre for Economic Studies and Planning, Jawaharlal Nehru University, New Delhi, India. Her research areas include globalization, international finance, employment patterns in developing countries, macroeconomic policy, and issues related to gender and development.

Professor Jayati Ghosh has held academic positions at Tufts University, Cambridge, and some institutions in India. She is one of the founders of the Economic Research Foundation in New Delhi, a non-profit trust devoted to progressive economic research. She is also Executive Secretary of the International Development Economics Associates (IDEAS), a network of economists critical of the mainstream economic paradigm of neo-liberalism.

She was the principal author of "The West Bengal Human Development Report" which has received the UNDP Prize for Excellence in Analysis. In addition to her many scholarly articles, she writes regular columns on economics and current affairs for the national magazine, *Frontline*, as well as *Businessline*, and the Bengali newspaper, *Ganashakti, Deccan Chronicle,* and *Asian Age.*

Professor Jayati Ghosh is a member of the National Knowledge Commission, advising the Prime Minister of India, and is closely involved in a range of progressive organisations and social movements. She has won several prizes and distinctions, such as the UNDP Award for Excellence in Analysis (for West Bengal Human Development Report) and the Ava Maiti Memorial Award (2004), the ILO Decent Work Research Prize (2010), and the NordSud Research Prize in Social Sciences (2010).

Some of her recent publications include: "The Indian economy 1970-2003", a chapter in *Cambridge Economic History of India, Vol. II,* (ed. S. Bhattacharya) New Delhi: Orient Longman, 2004; *Never Done and Poorly Paid: The changing nature of women's work in globalising India,* Women Unlimited:New Delhi, 2008; "The social and economic impact of financial liberalisation: A primer for developing countries", in Jose Antonio Ocampo and K.S. Jomo (eds) *Policy Matters*, Opus Books and Zed Books, 2008; *A Decade After: Crisis: Recovery and Adjustment in East Asia*, (with C. P. Chandrasekhar) Tulika Publishers, New Delhi, 2009.

Amadou Mahtar Mbow was born in 1921 in Dakar, Senegal. Early in life, he had adhered to certain principles, such as his religious beliefs and commitment to the Scout Movement, which made it easy for him to volunteer to fight in World War II. At the end of the war, he enrolled at the Sorbonne where he obtained his Bachelor's degree in History, and then joined the teaching profession. A true teacher, Amadou did a number of field research related to basic education and literacy, and published several textbooks on history and geography. He is a teacher and a militant. He contributed tremendously to the student movement in Senegal and the country's struggle for independence. He was Education and Culture Minister (1957–1958), Education Minister (1966–1968), and Youth Culture and Sports Minister (1968–1970) and lastly, Member of Parliament. Amongst others, he has also served as Deputy Director General UNESCO (1970-1974), and later Director General (1974–1987), during which his fight for a New World Order for Information and Communication (NOMIC) was highly recognized. One of his remarkable achievements is that he championed the publication of Africa's General History in eight volumes. Amadou Mahtar Mbow has received award of excellence (Doctor honoris causa) from about fifty different universities around the world. His ninetieth birthday anniversary was celebrated in May 2011 at the UNESCO headquarters in Paris.

Sam Moyo is a professor and the executive director of the African Institute for Agrarian Studies (AIAS) based in Harare, Zimbabwe. He has more than 28 years of research and lecturing experience on rural development issues with a focus on land reforms, agrarian change, environmental policy, and social movements. He has taught at the universities of Calabar and Port Harcourt in Nigeria, and at the University of Zimbabwe, and taken part in various international training programmes. He is currently an Adjunct Professor at University of Fort Hare in South Africa. He has worked as an Associate Professor at the Institute of Development Studies at the University of Zimbabwe and as a Director for the Southern African Regional Institute for Policy Studies (SARIPS) based in Harare, Zimbabwe.

He was Vice President of CODESRIA (1995-1998) and then President of CODESRIA (2008-2011). Sam Moyo has been involved in several major publications. Some of his recent publications include: *Reclaiming the Land: The Resurgence of Rural Movements in Africa, Asia and Latin America* [co-edited with Paris Yeros]; (London: Zed Books, 2005); *African Land Questions, Agrarian Transitions and the State: Contradictions of Neoliberal Land Reforms*, (CODESRIA Greenbook, Dakar: 2008); *Land and Sustainable Development in Africa* [co-edited with Kojo Sebastian Amanor] (London: Zed Books, 2008).

Ebrima Sall is the CODESRIA Executive Secretary since 2009. Before this appointment, he was Senior Programme Officer and Head of Research at CODESRIA. Earlier, he had taught and held senior positions in several institutions, including the Nordic Africa Institute (NAI), Uppsala, Sweden, where he was a senior researcher. He holds a PhD in Sociology from the University of Paris 1 Panthéon-Sorbonne (France). Some of his publications include: *Africa: Reaffirming Our Commitment* co-edited with Adebayo Olukoshi & Jean-Bernard Ouédraogo; *Human Rights and the Dilemmas of Democracy in Africa* (co-edited with Lennart Wohlgemuth); *Citizenship and Violence in Cote d'Ivoire* (co-edited with Jean-Bernard Ouedraogo); and *Women in Higher Education: Gender and Academic Freedom in Africa and the Social Sciences in Africa.*

Jomo Kwame Sundaram is a prominent Malaysian economist, who has served as the United Nations Assistant Secretary-General for Economic Development in the United Nations Department of Economic and Social Affairs (DESA) since 2005. He was founder Chair of International Development Economics Associates (IDEAs), and member of the Board of the United Nations Research Institute For Social Development (UNRISD), Geneva. In 2007, he was awarded the Wassily Leontief Prize for Advancing the Frontiers of Economic Thought. During 2008-2009, he served as adviser to Father Miguel d'Escoto Brockmann, President of the 63rd United Nations General Assembly, and as a member of the Stiglitz Commission of Experts of the President of the United Nations General Assembly on Reforms of the International Monetary and Financial System.

Jomo is a leading scholar and expert on the political economy of development, especially in Southeast Asia, who has published or co-edited over a hundred books and translated 12 volumes besides writing many academic papers and articles for the media. He is member of the editorial boards of several learned journals.

Born in Penang, Malaysia, in 1952, Jomo studied at the Penang Free School, Royal Military College, Yale and Harvard universities. He has taught at Science University of Malaysia (USM, 1974), Harvard (1974-1975), Yale (1977), National University of Malaysia (UKM, 1977-1982), University of Malaya (1982-2004) and Cornell (1993). He has also been a Visiting Fellow at Cambridge University (1987-1988; 1991-1992) and a Senior Research Fellow at the Asia Research Institute, National University of Singapore (2004).

Before joining the UN, Jomo was already widely recognized as an outspoken intellectual, with unorthodox non-partisan views. Before the Asian financial crisis in 1997-98, Jomo was an early advocate of appropriate new capital account management measures, which then Prime Minister Mahathir Mohamad later introduced. When then Deputy Prime Minister Anwar Ibrahim was imprisoned without trial under the Internal Security Act, Jomo publicly condemned the repression. In late 1998, he was sued for defamation for 250 million ringgit by Vincent Tan, a Mahathir era billionaire, who later dropped the case after almost a decade.

Introduction: Challenges and Opportunities

Ebrima Sall

The Council for the Development of Social Science Research in Africa, CODESRIA, held its 13th General Assembly, 5-9 December 2011, in Rabat, Morocco. The triennial General Assembly is one of the most important scientific events on the African continent. It provides the African social science research community with a unique opportunity to reflect on some of the key issues facing the social sciences in particular, and Africa and the world at large. The theme of the scientific conference for the 13th CODESRIA General Assembly was: "Africa and the Challenges of the Twenty-first Century".

The 21st century, like the previous one does not seem capable of breaking from the paradigm of the complex and the uncertain. Instead, it is confirming that hastily and carelessly proclaiming "the end of history", as Fukuyama did, was not enough to legitimately dispose of issues and challenges such as those of how to understand the presence of Africa in a world where emerging powers (Brazil, Russia, India, China and South Africa) are increasingly upsetting traditional global geopolitics.

The financial crisis and its social implications in some countries of the North and the increasingly global nature of many problems have raised awareness about the vital and imperious need for Africans to theoretically tackle the issue of Africa's future in this new century. This underscores the legitimacy of an approach that is founded on a rupture: a clean break with Afro-pessimism from outside and from within to show that the new global political and economic order is not a fatality but one that calls for a breaking off with a theoretical construction of Africa which led to the posing of questions like those asked by the World Bank in 2000: "Can Africa claim its place in the 21st century?"

It is about understanding why and how Africa is still at the heart of the new global political and economic strategies, and what opportunities there are for our continent to reposition itself in the world, and reposition the world with regard to its own objectives, perhaps the most important of which still remains that of bringing development (also to be understood as freedom, as Sen has argued) to its people.

It is also a question of deconstructing what some have called "the confinement of Africa in a rent economy" in order to more critically understand the opportunities available to the continent and also the constraints facing it, because the basic question is how, in the course of this 21st century, we can have a paradigm shift from the "invention of Africa" by the world to an "invention of the world" by Africa.

Global Issues, Global Challenges

Increasingly complex neoliberal globalization, changes in intercultural relations at the global level, climate change, poverty, rapid urbanization , the ICTs revolution, the emergence of knowledge societies, the evolution of gender and intergenerational relations, the evolution of spirituality and of the status and the role of religion in modern societies, the emergence of a multi-polar world and the phenomenon of emerging powers of the South are some of the realities of our world that are widely and extensively discussed by both academics and policy-makers. Some of these challenges have been identified in the 2010 and 2013 editions of the International Social Sciences Council's World Social Sciences Report, as major challenges of the 21st century.

Discussions on climate change, like those on the so-called emerging powers, are much more important today than they were 30 to 40 years ago. The Rio Summit on global environmental change was a key moment in the mobilization of the international community to face the challenges arising from global warming, such summits were rare. It inaugurated the long series of major international events, the most notable of which are the COPs, the Conference of the Parties to the UNFCCC, the 21st of which will be held in Paris in December 2015. Major international programmes on reducing greenhouse gas emissions, such as REDD and REDD+, have also been launched. Furthermore, the creation of the Euro Zone as well as the rise of countries like China and India, have also had repercussions worldwide.

The question one must ask is: How does all this affect Africa? And how prepared is the continent to face these challenges as well as those that will arise in the future? It is, nowadays, rather difficult to keep pace with advances in science and technology, including in the areas of biotechnology and nanotechnology, genetic engineering, etc. The challenge that Africa is facing is not only that of understanding how new scientific discoveries may have an impact on our societies, but also that of how to become a "continent of science" itself.

The rapidity of the pace of change in virtually all spheres of social life at the local, national, continental, and global levels make it difficult to identify the challenges that Africa will be facing in the coming century beyond a few decades. Science itself is changing as a result of changes occurring in nature and in society. Moreover, science and technology, far from being neutral, have become key players in the evolutions that occur in production systems, trade, and intercultural relations, as well as in research and the formulation of responses to environmental change. The ability of science to anticipate, read and interpret the processes of change has increased over the years. The ability of humanity to follow developments taking place in nature, and to capture the major trends taking place within society, is likely to increase as science itself develops. Therefore, the list of questions that can be considered as major challenges for the 21st century is likely to change over time.

Africa of the Twenty-first Century

Africa has entered the 21st century with huge unresolved issues, such as poverty, rapid urbanisation, the national question, regional integration, gender inequality, food insecurity, violent conflict, political fragmentation, and the fact of occupying a subaltern position in the global community, and in global governance. The weight of the past is a major handicap for Africa. The effects of the slave trade, colonization and neo-colonialism that Africa has suffered from are still being felt, as they have each and together resulted in the suppression of freedoms, the violation of human rights and dignity of the peoples of the continent, as well as the looting of human, natural and intellectual resources and led to what the pan-Africanist historian Walter Rodney called the "underdevelopment" of Africa.

Among the major disadvantages of the continent at the dawn of the 21st century are also the low level of education of many Africans, the lack of modern techniques of production, transport, etc.., a fragmented political space and the extrovert structure of the economies. The institutions of higher education and cultures of the elites are strongly marked, not by a philosophy and development strategies guided by the interests of African peoples, but by influences coming from the North, influences that are more alienating than liberating.

Nevertheless, the Africa of the end of the first decade of the 21st century is not exactly the same as the Africa of the early sixties which had just got freedom from colonial rule. The challenges the continent faces today are not exactly the same as those of the sixties. Although there are still issues dating back to the early years of independence, these are of a different order, and are today discussed with a particular focus and a sense of urgency. This is particularly true of the issues of governance and development, most of which are yet to be resolved.

Yet by all indications, these issues have gained particular relevance and magnitude. The celebration of the 50th anniversary of the independence of many countries in 2010 provided an opportunity for African researchers to review the continent's performance in 50 years of independence. There have been many achievements in terms of social and economic development. Enormous progress has been made in education and health, and some countries have managed to establish democratic governance systems, especially after the wave of national conferences (in West and Central Africa) at the end of the 1980s and early 1990s.

The fall of authoritarian regimes, the end of apartheid, the change of ruling parties in countries like Senegal, and the recent profound changes in Tunisia (the

"Jasmine Revolution"), Egypt and elsewhere in North Africa have made the promise of democratization and development of Africa much more real. Yet even with the recent political transformations, governance issues are still part of the great challenges facing our continent. Africa is still beset by the paradox of poverty in plenty: most people of the continent are poor despite the fact that the countries they live in are rich in human and natural resources.

Poverty is still massive and deeply rooted, and the processes that lead to exclusion and marginalization of large segments of African societies are still ongoing. Exclusion and political marginalization of individuals, groups and entire social classes are, as we know, among the root causes of many of the violent conflicts that have ravaged several African countries, while aggravating underdevelopment and international dependence.

Some of the "remedies" to the economic crisis and, more generally, to the problems of underdevelopment and widespread poverty that have been proposed or imposed on Africa have, in some cases contributed to the worsening of problems that they were supposed to solve. Others, like the use of genetically modified organisms (GMOs) as an antidote to food insecurity, or large scale land alienation in favour of multinational companies producing food crops or crops to obtain bio-fuels, raise significant political, ethical and health concerns, making the land question more complex.

Commodification, and attempts to subject almost all spheres of nature and society, including human organs, forest resources, and the social sciences themselves, to a market logic pose enormous challenges for science and for society, even if in some respects, the process has directed the flow of precious financial and human resources to some key issues and led to major discoveries that could enhance social progress. However, by all indications, with the exception of a few, the countries of the South are still at the level of receivers/consumers in the overall relationship that is behind these processes, or at best in the role of "passengers" rather than "drivers" of the process of globalization.

Reflections should also focus on issues such as the high mobility of African people, both within and outside the continent, and its consequences in terms of citizenship rights, as well as its impacts on gender relations; the issues of climate change, natural resource management and food security; the recurrent problem of African integration with a focus on the issue of a common currency and common borders; or yet again the governance of African cities, since a number of prospective studies have identified urbanization as a major trend in the evolution of the continent. These issues are likely to continue to determine the evolution of the continent.

Special attention should be paid to higher education, given the importance, and the uniqueness of the role that knowledge plays in development, and its ability to influence the whole system. Isn't the "vulnerability" of Africa the result of its marginal position in the world of knowledge? With the ongoing changes in higher education around the world and the weakening of many African universities as a result of both deep crises and years of structural adjustment, brain drain and sheer negligence on the part of the State, African research has encountered considerable difficulties in its attempts to study and interpret these events and more.

New technologies, especially ICTs play one of the most crucial roles in social, economic and political developments of the continent. For instance, the mobile phone and FM radio stations played an important role in the political and social movements in Senegal at the turn of the Millennium. Faced with restrictions on political debates in many countries such as Tunisia, we saw the importance of the internet, including social media and internet-based sites such as Facebook and Twitter as spaces for democratic struggles involving thousands of highly educated but unemployed urban youth. Meanwhile, the governance of the internet, a space managed mainly by private multinational companies of a new type (Facebook, Twitter, Google, YouTube, etc...), remains an unresolved issue.

Therefore the question is: Will this be Africa's century, as it is sometimes claimed? A better way to put more or less the same question is to ask: How can Africa take charge of its future and make this century the one of its renaissance? But what does it mean to make the 21st century the century of Africa and what does that imply? How could the social sciences and humanities address the challenges that we already know, and what types of improvements are required in the African higher education and research systems in order for them to better prepare Africa to face the challenges of the coming decades of this century? These are some of the questions that were also asked as the African Union (AU) led the celebration of the 50th anniversary of the Organisation of African Unity in 2013. The AU's *Agenda 2063* came out of this process (http://agenda2063.au.int/).

What is the role of intellectuals in general and CODESRIA in particular in addressing these challenges? The theoretical issues are very important. The production of knowledge informed by and that is relevant to the social realities in Africa has always been the ambition of CODESRIA and of all the great intellectuals of the continent. The intellectual struggles of Africa and the global South against the consequences of Western domination are far from having been won.

The scientific division of labour in which Africa is still mainly seen as a purveyor of raw materials of little use to the transformation of African societies is still in force. The epistemological agenda of the continent must continue to include the transformation of the dominant epistemological order which favours the West and penalizes the South, and Africa in particular. The valorization of the intellectual heritage and contributions of great thinkers from Africa and its Diaspora, must continue to be a part of our priorities. So must be the South-South and South-North dialogue.

The Casablanca Conference, 50 Years on

The 13th CODESRIA General Assembly took place shortly after many African countries had celebrated the fiftieth anniversary of their independence. It was also organised, 50 years after the 1961 Casablanca Conference that brought together Kwame Nkrumah (Ghana), Mwalimu Julius Nyerere (Tanzania), Gamal Abdel Nasser (Egypt), Ahmed Sekou Toure (Guinea), Modibo Keita (Mali), Ferhat Abbas (Algeria) and other leaders of newly independent African states and national liberation movements, to discuss the future of Africa. The "Casablanca Group", as they were known, formed the progressive camp. The Casablanca Conference which was hosted by King Mohammed V of Morocco, was a very important milestone in the process that led to the creation of the Organization of African Unity (OAU) in 1963. The fact that CODESRIA's 13th General Assembly was held in Morocco provided an opportunity for the African social science community to celebrate the fiftieth anniversary of this conference, and to pay tribute to the founding fathers and mothers of the OAU that was to become the African Union (AU) a few decades later, and ask the question as to how we can reinvigorate the African integration process, and renew our collective commitment towards realising the continental integration project.

This book contains the statutory lectures of the 13th General Assembly. Each one of them speaks to major challenges that Africa and the Global South are facing in this second decade of the 21st century: neoliberal globalization (Ghosh); capital flight (Sundaram); the land question (Moyo); gender relations with a particular focus on matriarchy (Amadiume); universalism (Mbow and Diagne). They also illustrate the multiple and often creative ways in which the social sciences and humanities are grappling with the major challenges that our societies are facing as transformations become more complex at every level, from the very local to the global.

1

The Challenges Facing Africa in the Twenty-first Century

Amadou Mahtar Mbow

First of all, I would like to thank the Executive Committee of CODESRIA, its President and its Executive Secretary, for inviting me to take the floor at this important General Assembly which brings together so many talented researchers from the African continent, its diaspora and other parts of the world, in order to discuss the problems of our common future. The social sciences can contribute enormously by shedding light on our path.

I should also like to express appreciation for the key role that CODESRIA has played since its inception in 1973 in developing the social sciences in Africa. The training that it has given, the meetings it has organised and the publications it has produced have greatly helped the social sciences to take root in the continent and to make progress. Without its activities, many important works by Africans could not have been undertaken or made accessible to other researchers, decision-makers and the general public.

The contribution of the social sciences seemed to me to be so important in obtaining knowledge about the factors that determine the workings of society that one of my first decisions when I took up my responsibilities as UNESCO's Director-General 36 years ago, was to create, for the first time in the Secretariat, a special sector for the social sciences, alongside the more traditional ones concerning education, the exact and natural sciences, as well as technology, culture and communication.

In fact, the social sciences, with which I associated the human sciences in general and philosophy, constitute a special instrument for knowledge and action. The aim was thus to give a place to their importance in international intellectual cooperation and in all the studies and research that could clarify the workings of societies and the world, in order to get a better understanding of them and to evaluate the action programmes and the various projects concerned with different aspects of life.

These included specific programmes concerning human rights, youth, gender and the status of women, peace, disarmament, population, urbanisation, the rural world and development in general, based on a multidisciplinary approach and concentrating on fields such as:

- The state of progress of the social sciences in the world, the reinforcement of national and regional institutions and support for research and training programmes;
- On the methodological level, the drawing up and implementation of tools that could promote the application of the social sciences, above all through socio-economic analysis, knowledge of situations, the planning and evaluation of action, particularly in the context of development;
- The concerted application of social sciences to understanding the most crucial social and human problems and the search for solutions to these problems, particularly in the fields of education, science, culture and communication.

A general principle that guided this programme's conception was, above all, to prioritise the endogenous development of the social sciences in order to promote the research and reflection within each society that was appropriate for enlightening them on their present and likely future situations, thus enriching and diversifying the basis of humanity's knowledge and wisdom.

There was also concern to promote complementarity between social science research, enriched by philosophical reflection, and human experience within each society. The multidimensional nature of social and human problems and all the relations between the great problems that today confront humanity also had to be borne in mind, particularly the complex, dialectical interactions between peace, disarmament, human rights and development in a world increasingly marked by the interdependence between nations and peoples.

And so, I willingly accepted to make a few modest reflections at the opening of CODESRIA's 13th General Assembly dedicated to 'Africa and the Challenges of the 21st Century'.

These challenges are the consequence of a long evolution in the world, of which you will first of all allow me to recall some essential facts. I refer to what is generally known today as globalisation. This corresponds, in my opinion, to a gradual Europeanisation of the world. It was, in fact, Europe, together with the countries resulting from the settling of Europeans in other parts of the world, who started this process and who, over centuries, obtained their prosperity from it, using labour and resources – of course, in different ways – from all other parts of the world.

The beginning of this process can be dated back to the 15th century, with the Renaissance in Europe, the birth of modern capitalism and circumnavigation round the world. The Renaissance freed philosophical reflection and scientific thought from the dominance and influence of the Church. There was a novel vision of mankind's relationships with nature, knowledge and society that gradually called into question many certitudes of the past. A new era was opened in all fields of creativity – artistic, literary and, above all, scientific and technical.

A freer climate contributed to the renewal of thought, based particularly on the ancient heritage of Greece that had been preserved, enriched and transmitted by the Muslim world. Then a profound renovation started in the economic and social fields, a renovation that stimulated a spirit of initiative and a desire to launch out.

At the same time this was the era of long-distance maritime navigation. It was promoted by the progress in naval construction and the adoption of new navigation instruments. More efficient ships could now plough the seas, driven by the needs for expansion of burgeoning modern capitalism that, century after century, made Europe the neuralgic centre of the world.

The Portuguese were the first to undertake maritime adventures along the African coasts. In 1444 they reached sub-Saharan Africa, arriving at the Cape Verde peninsula, site of the present city of Dakar. Year after year they made their way to the south of the continent and rounded the Cape of Good Hope, in present South Africa, reaching India in 1498. India was the country of origin of the spices that played an important role in trans-border commerce – spice consumption being very high in Europe. For their part the Spaniards were looking for India in a western direction and they arrived in 1492, with Christopher Columbus, in a continent hitherto unknown to the Europeans and which was later called America.

This, then, was how the way was paved for the immense undertaking of the domination and exploitation of the labour and resources of all the known world, by and for a Europe that was creative, dynamic and entrepreneurial and which then turned the whole planet into an open field for its economic, political and cultural expansion.

The destruction of the pre-Colombian states of America and the extermination of many indigenous people, as well as the importation of sub-Saharan Africans who had to submit to unremunerated forced labour, enabled nascent capitalism to benefit from massive profits from plantations and above all, from silver and gold mines. When I visited the Potosi silver mines not far from La Paz in Bolivia, I was reminded of a saying of Simon Bolivar, namely that the silver extracted from them could make it possible to construct a bridge that joined Latin America to Spain.

This shows what great wealth was extracted from the silver mines, at that time the most famous in the world. Thus, the primitive accumulation phase of capital, its reinforcement through the industrial revolution and the triangular trade involving African slaves all provided Europe, from the 16th to the early 19th century, with the financial resources and the necessary markets for its prodigious development. These resources were to increase still further with the colonial conquests and occupations of the 19th and 20th centuries.

In no way did the political independence of most of the American continent at the end of the 18th and the beginning of the 19th century put a brake on the Europeanisation of the world. It even consolidated it. The new states that were built up on the ruins of former colonies were essentially inspired by European ideology, which served as a basis for their struggles for emancipation, because of the origin and culture of their leaders that – apart from Haiti – determined their value systems and the forms of government that they set up. Hence, their economic and cultural ties with Europe, rather than diminishing, increased. New immigrants, adding to the old ones, were drawn from different parts of Europe into the new world.

On the cultural level, Europe was the only model and, on the economic level, the main supplier, the leading client and the chief investor. This continued up to the Second World War. The autochthonous people were excluded from political power almost everywhere until recently, when Morales, a pure bred Amerindian, was able to accede to power in Bolivia which, however, remained in the hands of those of European descent, who continue to be linked to Europe.

Indeed the end of direct colonial domination on the greater part of North and South America certainly did nothing to dampen the dynamism of European colonial imperialism. At the end of the 19th century and the beginning of the 20th, Europe, for economic, strategic and sometimes religious reasons, launched the almost total conquest of Africa and Oceania, as well as much of Asia. The fall of the Ottoman Empire after World War I, gave Europe a determining influence over the countries of the Middle East that were rich in oil and it attributed to itself, as well as to the United States, the exclusivity for exploiting this major source of energy for the new industrial revolution up until what is called 'the oil crisis', at the beginning of the 1970s.

The active exploitation of the resources of the countries that had been conquered, often without any concern for their human and ecological consequences, supplied the expansion of European industries with cheap raw materials, special access to markets and possibilities for lucrative investments by financial capital. These somewhat attenuated the effects of the cyclical economic crises of the second half of the 19th and the beginning of the 20th century in Europe.

As far as Africa is concerned, I shall not talk about the dramatic consequences on its populations and social structures of forced labour, the obligatory cultivation of crops and the requirement to supply products such as rubber. I only want to emphasise that the African peasants and workers became, willingly or unwillingly, the suppliers of basic products for an international trade in full expansion and the tools of an accumulation of a not negligible part of the resources that promoted the progress of the economies of the colonial countries at the height of their industrialisation. This took place in the same way that their ancestors had achieved the primitive accumulation phase of capitalism at the beginning and during the expansion of modern capitalism, with the slave trade and triangular commerce.

At the start of the 20th century, European ships were criss-crossing the seas of the whole world, transporting merchandise of all kinds and taking to their ports all that contributed to the prosperity and well-being of Europe. European finance invested everywhere where it could prosper, while European armed forces, reinforced by indigenous back-up troops, were everywhere on land and sea in all those parts of the world where European interests were at stake. European languages and cultures were increasingly adopted by the elites in all continents.

It could be said then, that the globalisation that had been under way since the end of the 15th century and the beginning of the 16th had taken a decisive step. It is true that World War I politically and financially weakened Europe, which was soon replaced by the United States of America, but its resonance remained intact all over the world. The new states that had come out of Europe emerged with a certain prosperity. They had special relationships with Europe, which reinforced its presence, thus contributing to the Europeanisation of the world: the synonym of globalisation.

Globalisation process accelerated with the World War II. This war, in which nations of all continents participated, showed, through the huge destruction and loss of human lives, that it had caused the dangers that humanity was incurring through fragmentation and conflicts. Hence efforts were made, through the Bretton Woods agreement, then the adoption of the United Nations Charter at San Francisco and the creation of the UN system, to affirm 'the common solidarity of humanity' and to seek to ensure the maintenance of peace and security, and to promote the 'common prosperity of humanity'.

This is the context of the struggles undertaken for the emancipation of the countries that had been colonised in a world in which Europe was weakened, but still had a certain influence. The United States then became the dominant power, especially after the end of the Cold War.

In some cases, independence was acquired following negotiations, while in others it was after bloody struggles, which were intensified by the interference of the great powers in what was called the Cold War. However, it was very hot in the countries of the South: those struggles brought about the deaths of hundreds of thousands, if not millions of deaths and great destruction.

Indeed, the emergence of new nations on the international scene, demographic growth, a considerable increase in the production of goods and services, thanks especially to scientific and technical advances, created the conditions for an amazing multiplication of relations of all kinds between nations and peoples. The future of contemporary societies thus seemed to take place in a space that expanded the dimensions of the planet.

This can be seen from the expansion of international trade, the temporary international flows of migration through tourism and studies in far-distant countries, as well as permanent flows through the displacement of workers towards the highly-productive regions. The exchange of messages, information and immaterial goods, through communication satellites and the Internet, experienced a growth which has largely overtaken that of world trade in raw materials and finished products.

Societies that were able to live for a long time almost totally unaware of each other found themselves increasingly in close contact. Reciprocal influences multiplied and interdependence, in fact, became multidimensional. It was certainly a source of mutual enrichment, an opening up of initiative and creativity, but also of frustration, as its progress created many inequalities, the worsening of conditions for certain peoples, the restriction of margins for manoeuvre, an increase in unpredictability and greater vulnerability. There has been growing poverty – so frequent in the developing countries – while even in the industrialised countries increasing numbers of people are now living precariously.

Moreover, decisions taken by states in certain fields have had to take into account an ever-growing number of factors that are outside their control and these decisions, in turn, can have various degrees of repercussions outside their own borders. This can be seen with the financial crisis that has prevailed over the last few years, forcing many countries to take draconian measures that are not easily endured by the most disadvantaged sections of the population.

Also, the economic strategies of many countries are more and more governed by the logic of a competition that is carried out at world level, a logic that symbolises the internationalisation of the production and capital of transnational corporations. This internationalisation has harmful effects on all societies, and the risks cannot be ignored by specialists in the social sciences whose mission it is to evaluate the nature of these risks and their consequences, as well as to advocate norms that can attenuate them.

In fact, the activities of some inflict ecological damage on others, as with the oil spills in the seas, increased greenhouse gases in the atmosphere and the threats of nuclear contamination. These risks are spreading to more and more zones and will last for an inconceivably long period – not to mention the climatic modifications that seem linked to a certain extent to human activity.

This is, I believe, the context for any reflection on the challenges that Africa has to face in this 21st century that some have predicted will be the African century, the one in which its peoples will emerge from the long night during which it had lost all control over itself and its resources.

These global challenges concern the whole planet: climate change, the degradation of the environment, the drying up of certain natural resources such as those in fresh water and those of the sea, the nuclear danger, the threat to peace and the security of nations, and misunderstanding of all kinds that lead to serious conflicts. These cannot be ignored by Africa and it is obliged to contribute in resolving them with the rest of the human community. But it also has specific challenges linked to its history, which I would like to emphasise. These challenges are many and various; they are at one and the same time political, economic social and cultural.

The political challenges are the consequence of the colonial carving up, the conditions of access to independence, the nature of the new institutions and the way they function. Colonisation had brought various populations together in one administrative body and in an authoritarian manner. They had different languages and traditions. The diverse colonial forces were careful to stop any questioning of this state of things, violently repressing all efforts to challenge the established order.

Once independence was acquired, conflicts broke out, sometimes incited from outside and often of an ethnic nature. In most sub-Saharan African states, centrifugal forces became increasingly active, both to contest the legitimacy of established power, particularly contesting the way in which it had taken over the control of the state machinery, as well as denouncing its economic and social policy and protesting against the corruption and favouritism that favoured one or several ethnic or other groups close to the leaders, to the detriment of others.

What is at stake in these conflicts is mostly the acquisition of power or, at least, its sharing, without challenging membership of the same state. However, some of these conflicts have had, or are still in the process of having, clearly separatist objectives. This was the case at the dawn of independence of the former Belgian Congo, with Katanga; and then Nigeria, with a terrible civil war, resulting from the separation of the eastern province that proclaimed itself the Republic of Biafra (1967-1970).

These two uprisings ended in failure but others succeeded such as, for example, the case of Eritrea and South Sudan, which became independent states. Elsewhere, the after-effects of the recent confrontations in Côte d'Ivoire and, to a lesser extent, in Senegal with the Casamance, are still fresh in our memories.

Thus, the main political challenge has been one of national integration and democracy. Integration should enable each individual, each ethnic group, and each social category to become aware of its membership in solidarity with the national community in which it finds itself. Not only are the rights of everyone to be recognised and respected on an equal level but the problem of reinforcing the unity and cohesion of the nation is also a common concern.

As for democracy it requires stable institutions that are known in all the languages spoken by the populations and not changeable at will, as well as transparent and honest elections. It must be a participatory democracy in countries that are in the process of construction, with the commitment of everyone who, being aware of what is at stake, can guarantee the success of what is being done to accelerate a development that benefits everyone and not just a few. This is a vast field where the social sciences can make a substantial contribution through comparative case studies, in order to promote sound norms and practices in conformity with the requirements of real national unity.

Development is another major challenge. It should be noted, in this respect, that Africa participates relatively little in world trade. It imports a large part of the equipment, food and finished goods that it needs and it exports mostly oil and minerals, without benefiting much from the added value. Thus, there is the basic problem of a revaluation of its production and a total reorientation of its economy in function of the needs and aspirations of its populations.

There is little point in stressing the poverty that, after fifty years of independence, is the lot of a large part of the populations of Africa. This poverty takes the form of malnutrition; health care that is not equally accessible, above all for the poorer sectors of society; unhealthy housing, particularly in the *banlieus* of the big cities that are crammed by those fleeing from the precariousness of the rural areas; and unemployment which affects so many young people who have no university training. This is the result of bad development, characterised especially by family agriculture which is far from meeting satisfactorily the requirements of populations that are rapidly increasing, or from supplying the surpluses that promote new investment and give work to the young, who see their only salvation in rural exodus or trying to emigrate to other continents. It is also a development that is characterised by a grossly insufficient industrialisation and a service sector that is often under external control. When young people have no other alternative than to flee their countries at the peril of their lives to look elsewhere for the means to survive, leaders must pose themselves serious questions as to whether they are capable of conducting their nations along the path to development and the well-being of all.

Development also involves the training of people through a generalised educational system that provides prospects for everyone: a system that is conceived, not in imitation of others but oriented to respond to the cultural context and national needs; an education that promotes the scientific mind and scientific and technical training, as well as the research and the development research that is indispensable for the changes in the production and service sectors.

One of the main challenges for Africa remains, in fact, the appropriation of science and techniques and its participation in research in all fields with a view to increasing the capacity for innovation of its researchers and its engineers. At independence, Africa had been left behind and, since then, while in general there has been some progress, it must be recognised that it falls far short of the requirements for modern development. Not long ago, statistics revealed that Africa is the poorest continent in terms of skilled personnel in the field of research and development research. The number of scientific and technical specialists working in the field of research and development research was 25 times less than the average in the industrialised countries. The percentage of the gross domestic product (GDP) that is devoted to research is six times below the world average. As a proportion of its population, Africa has ten times fewer scientists than the world average.

I do not think that these figures have changed very much. Few African countries have been able to define an adequate scientific and technical policy and implement it with the appropriate means. As happened for a long time in Europe, scientific research is concentrated in the universities. But many of them do not fulfil this function very well because of lack of means. A number of universities seem to favour theoretical training to the detriment of research activities – research that is oriented towards solving the problems of today's Africa.

The training that is given in many universities does little to promote the emergence of scientific communities in sufficient numbers in the most essential branches of knowledge. This is not to overlook the social and human sciences, whose role in elucidating the problems confronting societies that are rapidly changing cannot be exaggerated. But the importance given to the exact and natural sciences and the engineering sciences must be increased everywhere.

There is another challenge of vital importance to preserve the independence and integration of the continent. Divided as Africa is into many states of which a number are not very viable in the world of today, its integration becomes an imperative need. United and combining its different potentialities, Africa, a continent of the future, should be able to hope for a better destiny. If it is divided, it will remain weak and dependent on external interests. The unity mystique is not a utopia because if it depends on the will of the people: it can give hope to hundreds of millions of young people created by the demographic explosion emerging in our cities and rural areas.

The Casablanca conference that took place in 1961 was one of the first initiatives to be taken on the path towards integration. This took place in a particular context, marked especially by the events in the Congo, which showed how the colonial powers, while accepting the constraints imposed by decolonisation, tried to conserve all the privileges they had previously enjoyed by maintaining their strategic, economic, financial, commercial and cultural interests. They even sought to claim the right to intervene in choosing leaders and dictating to them how to govern their countries.

Hence, at the Casablanca conference there were numerous recommendations that opposed the budding neo-colonialism in order to complete the total liberation of the continent in which the liberation movements were still leading horrific wars for independence in several countries, for the suppression of *apartheid* and all racist practices. The participants at this conference felt that Africa would not be truly independent until these conditions were achieved. They decided to reinforce their solidarity so that the better endowed countries aided those who were less endowed in order to avoid all possible interference from outside. They set up a secretariat to coordinate activities in different sectors, particularly in the military field.

The conference was followed, two years later, by the creation of the OAU. The special role that it played in achieving decolonisation and supporting the struggle against *apartheid* cannot be overemphasised.

The challenges mentioned above are not the only ones and others can be added. I will leave it at that, however, with just one last observation or, if you prefer to call it, challenge – and it is not the least important. It is the obligation of African intellectual elite, enriched by their different experiences in the world, from now on to think for themselves about the problems of the continent, freeing themselves from all external, alienating influences and ideologies. One cannot meet challenges without being aware of their exact nature and their real importance in the future of a society and take into account all its realities, such as the constraints of its past.

Africa will never emerge from the predicaments that it has experienced since independence unless its governing elites do not get rid of their tendency to look outside the continent for inspiration for their activities. It is in ourselves, in our abilities, to analyse and reflect, in our determination to act for the common good, that we must find the inspiration and strength necessary to undertake, together with our people, the changes that will lead to the stability and the well-being of all. I do not doubt that the intellectuals who have gathered here are animated by the same conviction and will act in this sense.

So I should like to end here, thanking you for your attention and wishing you every success in your work.

2

Development in a Turbulent World

Jayati Ghosh

Over the past few decades, there have been dramatic and even transformative changes in the global economy and in certain regions or countries. Nevertheless, for most African countries – and, indeed, for most countries in other continents – the basic problems of development just do not seem to get solved. In the simplest economic terms, development relates to the shift from lower to higher value economic activities, thereby raising aggregate productivity and per capita incomes through a process of productive diversification. This economic process is meant to be accompanied by improvements in social indicators that raise quality of life and expand the potential of societies to deliver human freedom. The constraints that prevent such a process from unfolding in any societies may vary, and they may change over time, but they still remain compelling (and, in some cases, binding) for much of the world.

The first decade of the new millennium was enlivened by new opportunities that generated a phase of relatively rapid aggregate GDP growth in most of the developing world. But by the early years of the second decade, some of these positive possibilities already seem to be diminishing, as demand for developing country exports slowed down with negative multiplier effects in many countries. We are, therefore, in a world economy that is changing so rapidly that analyses and projections based on available data on the past may fail to capture the current tendencies: by the time we are able to identify a clear trend, it may already be too late! This makes the tasks of designing and implementing economic policies for development much more complicated and requiring nimbleness of strategies and institutions, which is not so commonly found. Universal and homogenising principles based on simplistic intellectual models to determine such strategies – as exhibited, for example, in the 'Washington Consensus' – are, therefore, even less relevant today than they have ever been.

One important feature of the current international situation is the (still incipient) change in global power and global markets. The emergence of finance capital as a dominant and dominating player in global capitalism has been widely recognised for some time, and its implications continue to be severe for the developing world. But the past two decades has been seen as the period of 'emergence' of some developing countries as major exporters and importers, as well as new sources of foreign capital flows. In Africa, for example, China has not only become the dominant trading partner for most countries but also now accounts for the greater share of foreign capital inflows (in the form of aid, loans and direct investment). This is widely perceived to have significant implications for existing trade structures and patterns, as well as for global power as expressed in other ways. This in turn has led to the perception that it is possible for the developing world led by China (and to a lesser extent some of the other BRICS) to 'decouple' from the stagnating Northern economies.

There is no doubt that the world economy is changing and older power imbalances are shifting to newer and more complex scenarios. But a premature celebration of this tendency in 'emerging' economies, without careful recognition of the realities and limitations inherent in the process, is not only unjustified but can even be described as hubris. This is true firstly because recent trends have confirmed what was evident in 2008 and 2009 – that export dependence on northern economies is still critical for almost all developing countries, including the most 'dynamic'. And since so many developing countries are highly trade-dependent and have generally chosen export-oriented growth as the model, the slowdown in exports will necessarily also affect levels of economic activity, employment and future investment. But it is also true that expectations of future growth that continue to rely on the dominant neoliberal economic policy model are misplaced because this is unlikely to deliver sustained growth in future.

Limits to the Current Neoliberal Growth and Development Strategy

There are at least three considerations that make the current strategy of choice (even in the 'successful' developing countries) one that is hard to sustain in future: the impact of financial liberalisation; the mercantilist obsession with export-oriented growth that generates adverse distributive consequences; and the inadequate attention to ecological imbalances that are already evident and emerge from the patterns of material expansion.

Financial liberalisation has resulted in an increase in financial fragility in developing countries, making them prone to periodic financial and currency crises. These relate both to internal banking and related crises, and currency crises stemming from more open capital accounts. The origin of several crises can be traced to the shift to a more liberal and open financial regime, since this unleashes a dynamic that pushes the financial system towards a poorly regulated, oligopolistic structure, with a corresponding increase in fragility. Furthermore, liberalisation dismantles the very financial structures that are crucial for sustained economic growth, as it aggravates the inherent tendency in private markets to direct credit to non-priority and import-intensive but more profitable sectors, to concentrate investible funds in the hands of a few large players and to direct savings to already well-developed centres of economic activity. When it does lead to growth this typically is not a sustainable strategy because growth based on credit bubbles does not last – it leads to financial crisis and 'lost' periods.

Second, the paradigm of growth that has dominated has been that of seeing export-led activities as the fundamental engine of expansion. This is clearly no longer possible to the same extent. Europe is not going to be a source of new demand in the medium term. The United States is also unlikely to generate net additional demand for developing countries because even as it recovers slowly it is basing that recovery on domestic rebalancing that shrinks the size of its current account deficit and emphasises the 'inshoring' of more activities in manufacturing and the services sectors. Japan's current attempts at domestic economic revival through reflation do not imply a big increase in import demand and also have the impact of depreciating its currency, while the associated financial outflows are in the nature of hot money that can be easily reversed. So these Northern economies will reduce their imports from developing countries (DCs) through decline in domestic demand, contraction, protectionism, etc. In this context, putting all hopes on China as the new engine of growth for the developing world is misplaced because Chinese growth itself has been greatly dependent on Northern markets.

One significant feature of the past two decades has been significantly increased inequality – between countries and within a significant number of countries. Recent economic growth has been associated with and even depended upon the greater power of capital (both multinational and domestic), reflected in rising shares of profit and interest in national income. Governments have not seen higher wages, more employment and better conditions as economic policy priorities, but rather as eventual by-products of the growth process. Unfortunately, in many economies, income growth has not necessarily been accompanied by more good quality employment. Also, this profit-led growth is not sustainable beyond a point, as has become increasingly evident in the past few years. These poor employment outcomes (which also included higher rates of open unemployment in the past-crisis trajectory) were the result of deflationary policies on the part of the governments of these countries, which sought to suppress domestic consumption and investment. The 'excess savings' that were generated as a result were then stored as foreign exchange reserves – partly as insurance again future crises and partly to prevent exchange rate appreciation that would damage the export-driven model. This obviously had effects on current levels of economic activity relative to the potential. But it also negatively affected future growth prospects because of the long-term potential losses of inadequate infrastructure investment, etc.

This strategy bred and increased global inequality, and also sowed the seeds of its own destruction for both external and internal reasons. Externally, deficit countries will either choose or be forced to reduce their deficits through various means, including protectionist responses. Internally, suppression of wage incomes and domestic consumption is increasingly meeting with political resistance. In either case, the pressures to find more sustainable sources of economic growth, particularly through domestic demand and wage-led alternatives, are likely to increase.

The patterns of production and consumption that emerged meant that growth also involved rapacious and ultimately destructive exploitation of the environment. Climate change together with its adverse impact is only one of the pressing issues of concern: the other evident environmental costs in terms of excessive congestion, environmental pollution and ecological degradation are already being felt in most developing countries. The ecological constraints on such growth are already being felt, most unfairly, among those regions and groups of people that have gained the least from the overall expansion of incomes.

Development Strategies for the Future

It is evident that some fundamental questions that have been part of development concerns for at least two centuries still remain crucial. First, is the agrarian question and the issue of land in its various and changing manifestations. Second, and very much related to the first, is how to approach property relations and distribution. Third, the basic process of development as one of structural change and economic diversification has not disappeared, and must still be addressed. And finally, of course, is achieving the economic and social rights of all citizens, including the provision of basic needs through public provision, which is still the significant goal.

But all of these need to be defined and refined in relation to contemporary problems and possibilities. For developing countries there are clearly some new opportunities. Changed economic configurations and geopolitical shifts have operated to loosen and, in some cases, remove traditional forms of international control and inequality. Sometimes these have been replaced by newer forms, and sometimes they have meant a change in economic relationships. This does not mean that traditionally exploitative economic relations have vanished, but that there may be more space to negotiate within them. Meanwhile newer forms of exploitation are constantly being developed, especially because the policy context in most of the world is still very much one that privileges capital and emphasises market power over human rights.

Demographic changes and the significant presence of a large body of young people in many developing countries are frequently cited as a major advantage because of its association with lower dependency ratios. But it is also a major –

and quite possibly the dominant – challenge in the medium term. It means that a focus on employment generation as the central goal has become an urgent requirement, especially because across the developing world we have more and more educated youth even as there are fewer employment possibilities. The young are less likely to be patient about this imbalance, especially if there are no signs of better prospects in the medium term.

So we need new models of economic expansion and development that break from the currently dominant paradigm. This does not mean going back to large statist strategies that were regarded as overcentralised and inflexible. Rather, new wage and employment-led development strategies should be based on expanding livelihood possibilities, improving the viability and productivity of small producers and ensuring social and economic rights for all citizens. Such a strategy would, therefore, have two legs: reliance on strength of small producers, and massive increase in public social spending that delivers a diversifying potential. As Thandika Mkandawire has noted, social policy can be a means of lubricating and allowing development transformations, and can even be a cause or mechanism of development. Because of its role as countercyclical buffer, in creating new sources of demand and its significant multiplier effects, social policy should not be seen in simplistic terms as a welfare measure but rather as a macroeconomic strategy for growth.

A critical and necessary feature of progressive social policy is univeralism in provision and in entitlements. Targeting is prone to far too many errors of unfair exclusion and unjustified inclusion. Universalism creates a political constituency for good quality public provision. Such universal entitlements are also very important from a gender perspective, because women who perform huge amounts of unrecognised and unrewarded work for society within and outside their households otherwise tend to be excluded from forms of social protection that are provided to recognised paid workers. All this, therefore, creates greater social balance and equity and equality of opportunity.

This can be part of a broader policy of fiscal stimulation that is increasingly essential in both developed and developing countries, to cope with the adverse real economic effects of the ongoing crisis and prevent economic activity and employment from falling. Fiscal expenditure is also required to undertake and promote investment to manage the effects of climate change and promote greener technologies. And public spending is crucial to advance the development project in the South and fulfil the promise of achieving minimally acceptable standards of living for everyone in the developing world. The inevitable question is how this can be afforded. Fiscal strategies that are based on progressive taxation are obviously required.

Further, this necessarily requires the containment of finance, making it subservient to citizens. The current domination of finance is based on political economy that has to, that must and that will change. Obviously much greater and more comprehensive regulation of financial activity is required. In addition, ultimately, there is no alternative to systematic state regulation and control of finance. Since private players will inevitably attempt to circumvent regulation, the core of the financial system – banking – must be protected, and this is only possible through social ownership. Therefore, some degree of socialisation of banking (and not just socialisation of the risks inherent in finance) is also inevitable. In developing countries this is also important because it enables public control over the direction of credit, without which no country has industrialised.

All this must be combined with more ecologically sustainable patterns of production and distribution, and particularly urbanisation. Developing new means of measuring genuine progress, well-being and quality of life are very important. Quantitative GDP growth targets, which still dominate the thinking of regional policy makers, are not simply distracting from these more important goals, but can even be counterproductive. For example, a chaotic, polluting and unpleasant system of privatised urban transport involving many private vehicles and over-congested roads actually generates more GDP than a safe, efficient and affordable system of public transport that reduces vehicular congestion and provides a pleasant living and working environment. So it is not enough to talk about 'cleaner, greener technologies' to produce goods that are based on the old and now discredited pattern of consumption. Instead, we must think creatively about such consumption itself, and work out which goods and services are more necessary and desirable for our societies.

3

The Political Economy of Transformation in Zimbabwe: Radicalisation, Structural Change and Resistance[1]

Sam Moyo

Introduction: Radicalisation, Structural Change and Reform

The dynamics of the world economic crises at the turn of this century have evoked a new generation of radicalisms across the globe, including the so-called Arab Spring. Notwithstanding their distinctive characteristics related to their varied specific conditions, radical movements have been innovative in confronting universal social and political challenges. Zimbabwe's Fast Track Land Reform Programme (FTLRP), which officially began in 2000, is one such experience of radical reform which redressed settler-colonial land dispossession and racialised inequalities. Despite the resultant social and structural transformation, and the scope for a progressive development agenda and democratisation it represents, the land reform was widely dismissed as a case of African 'despotism', and subjected to 'regime change'. This was not surprising given the pervasiveness of neoliberal triumphalism, and the persistent dominance of social theories that characterise the African experience with little regard for historical context and the evolving social facts on the ground.

Zimbabwe does not represent an 'ideal type' model of reform or one which deserves uncritical emulation. It is not a model of socialist revolution, for it did not result in one (Moyo and Yeros 2005, 2007a, 2011b). Nor can we teleologically foreclose the long-term socio-political character of the outcome. Rather, it represents one of the rare instances of political and economic radicalisation which resulted in a redistributive outcome due to innovative socio-political mobilisation processes, interventionist state reforms and ongoing resistance, notwithstanding its attendant social and political contradictions. Yet, little scholarly attention was paid to the political and economic origins of the social crisis that triggered the radicalisation (Moyo 2001; Moyo and Yeros 2005), and to the wider implications of the outcomes of the Zimbabwean reforms for the subcontinent (see Moyo and Yeros 2007a and b).

The roots of the radicalisation in Zimbabwe lie in persistent local and national resistances to the racially structured model of capitalist accumulation achieved through colonial conquest from 1890. Extensive social displacement and territorial segregation, the super-exploitation of local and regional labour, and discriminatory agrarian policies, had represented an extreme social injustice. This condition was not redressed by the decolonisation pact of Zimbabwe in 1980, while the neoliberal economic policies adopted from 1990 exacerbated the situation, which degenerated into social crisis (Moyo 2000). This, in turn, provoked labour protests and galvanised popular land occupations which fuelled the radical nationalist reforms which escalated from 1997 (see Moyo 2001).

Radicalisation in Zimbabwe entailed confrontation by an array of social forces (classes) with settler-colonial power structures, capital and imperialism. The process escalated through the contradictions of a revolutionary situation, including an internal reconfiguration of political mobilisation in the former settler colony, and against external sanctions and political destabilisation. It entailed experimentation with a new economic structure with a diversified set of external economic relationships and continued resistance through new forms of rural mobilisation, indigenisation initiatives and a foreign policy based on positive non-alignment. The anti-colonial land movement blended with contemporary resistance movements in the contemporary context of primitive accumulation, highlighting the centrality of the emancipatory dimensions of the agrarian question, rather than the economic concerns often associated with agrarian reform (see Moyo, Jha and Yeros 2013).

This experience represents an example of resistance emerging out of the social crises generated by neoliberalism within a small country of apparently limited geo-strategic importance, other than its integral value as a former settler-colonial beachhead of imperialism, endowed with extensive mineral resources. Zimbabwe has rowed against the current scramble for African land, mineral resources, energy and consumer markets, at a time of significant material changes at the world system-level. Indeed, new geo-strategic facts are being established on the ground, in relation to the rising involvement of 'emerging powers' in competition for resource control, as well as the re-militarisation of US strategy in Africa (see Moyo, Jha and Yeros 2012; and Yeros forthcoming). While progressive internal reforms invite aggressive external interventions and polarise politics, the experience shows that innovative national and regional responses can be mobilised effectively in their defence against Western aggression and monopoly finance capital. Foreign policy was effectively used to mobilise regional solidarity and support, capitalising on the room of manoeuvre created by the rise of China (Moyo and Yeros 2013).

Intellectual authority over the narrative on Zimbabwe's land reform remains contested with regard to the causes, the nature and effects of the land reforms. Eurocentric perspectives, which rely on the ubiquitous organising concept of 'neopatrimonialism', in which the only relationship that exists in society is between rapacious black capitalists and their ethnicised client networks, held sway for a while (Moyo and Chambati 2013). Failing to understand the contradictions of Zimbabwe's radicalisation, such 'authorities' only saw a 'destructive party accumulation project' (Raftopoulos 2010:706) and not the radicalisation of various forces, including the semi-proletariat and aspiring black bourgeoisie, against monopoly capital. Various intellectuals and the Western media took recourse to racialised discourses of 'corruption' and 'orchestration', and vilified the whole of the land movement (see Johnson 2009), alleging that only the political elites benefited from the reforms.

The fact that the outcome was extensively redistributive, despite the disproportionate gains of some elites and the retention of some large-scale foreign-owned agro-industrial estates and conservancies, was posited earlier on (e.g. Moyo and Yeros 2005; Moyo *et al.* 2009; Moyo 2010), but this is only recently being corroborated as a novel outcome (Scoones, *et al.* 2010; Matondi 2013; Hanlon *et al.* 2013). Although a full recovery of agricultural output to the 1990s levels (which ought not to be seen as ideal targets) is slowly coming to fruition, the reforms continue to face various internal and external political and economic constraints (Moyo and Nyoni 2013). However, agrarian relations have improved substantially, with agrarian labour relations having been diversified within the new land tenure relations (Chambati 2013) and the scope for smaller producers on some markets having been opened wide, as popular participation in and benefits from the wider agrarian economy grow (Moyo and Nyoni 2013).

Despite the emerging consensus on some of the basic outcomes, there remain important differences in our understanding of the political and socio-economic implications of the reform, and the policies required to progressively advance popular welfare. Neopatrimonial perspectives which obscure the structural power of monopoly-finance capital, because they reduce all social relations to localised and ethnicised categories of domination and resistance, continue to argue for further market liberalisation to counter state interventions. Liberal populist frameworks applaud the new livelihoods being realised as evidence of autonomous peasant' agency *vis-a-vis* the state (Scoones *et al.* 2010) obviating the need for enhanced interventions, and highlight the fact that some black farmers are doing as well as the previous white farmers without the privileges derived from state subsidies (Hanlon *et al.* 2013). Others persist in their belief that the return of private property relations will stimulate recovery (Matondi 2012), despite the limits imposed by the external squeeze on the economy.

The systemic role of monopoly capital and extroverted markets in shaping the emerging uneven accumulation trajectory and the absence of credit for food cropping, as the re-insertion of big capital into the new agrarian structure ensues, tends to be glossed over (Moyo 2011b; Moyo and Chambati 2013). The new market contradictions that have emerged from price repression inscribed in the growth of contract farming in the capitals from the East and West, as well as domestic white and black capital compete to capture the new landholders' products, suggesting the need for renewed state interventionism. Yet, the importance of recent state interventions in favour of small and new producers is being occluded in emerging discourses which argue for competitiveness on world markets (despite their volatility), and decry the 'evils' of 'dependence' on state 'subsidies' (USAID 2012). Thus, accumulation from below remains constricted, and new forms of social differentiation increasingly polarise the benefits of the reform.

Four aspects of the results of research conducted on the FTLRP since 2000 by a range of scholars, under the rubric of the African Institute of Agrarian Studies (see Moyo and Chambati 2013), and their implications for reform elsewhere, are discussed namely:

- The coordinated mobilisation of a national land movement for land reform, beyond the erstwhile market and bureaucratic framework, through a multi-class, decentralised and anti-bureaucratic formation, united by radical nationalism;
- A process of structural reform that sought, as a matter of state policy, the accommodation of various social forces as concretised in a tri-modal outcome of land distribution, leading to competing modes of agrarian production;
- The re-configuration of agrarian markets through state intervention to sustain the recovery of production, despite the resurgence of social differentiation and competing accumulation strategies; and
- The emergence of new rural movements seeking progressive agrarian reforms and indigenous control of natural resources, in the recent context of the scramble for Africa resources.

Historical context of the Fast Track Land Reform

To understand the radicalisation of Zimbabwe after its neoliberal turn in the 1990s, the nature of capitalist agrarian accumulation and the character of the decolonisation pact must be clarified. Racial monopolistic control over land, water resources, farm subsidies, and public infrastructural investments had by 1930 established about 6000 white settlers on large-scale 'commercial' farms based on private property relations. Their accumulation trajectory derived from the super-exploitation of migrant labour from the reserves created at the expense of African peasantries relegated to marginal lands (Amin 1972), and discriminatory agrarian markets and subsidies. From the 1950s, the accumulation trajectory was augmented by the creation of large-scale agro-industrial estates, also heavily subsidised by the state (Moyo 2010). By 1970, Zimbabwe's bimodal landholding structure, based on the incomplete dispossession of peasant lands, had resulted not in creating 'enclaves', but a functional dualism which repressed labour and peasant farming. Farm output had shifted from peasant food production towards export commodities and urban markets, dominated by large farmers in alliance with state marketing boards and monopoly capital. This accumulation model was in crisis by 1975, following the oil crisis and the escalating liberation war.

Since decolonisation in Southern Africa was delayed in the 1960s, a combination of armed and political struggle led to military victories in the Lusophone territories, and negotiated transitions from 1980 in Zimbabwe, 1990 in Namibia, and 1994 in South Africa. An integrated, thirty-year regional conflict, involving the destabilisation of the region by the Apartheid regime in South Africa, saw aggression being used as a lever of negotiation, until the whole region succumbed to a generalised pact in the 1990s, at the close of the cold war (Moyo and Yeros 2013). This entailed peace, independence and majority rule, in return for property guarantees, and economic opening to monopoly and finance capital, such that decolonisation and neoliberalism coincided; the one being conditional on the other (*ibid*). The Anglo-American guarantors of the Zimbabwe negotiations promised financing for the proposed market-led land redistribution programme, but such support was limited (Moyo 1999).

The pact was always unstable, despite the defeat of previous plans which had sought to retain white political privileges indefinitely. In Zimbabwe, some in the nationalist movement led by the Patriotic Front parties (ZANU-PF and PF-ZAPU), viewed the pact as a strategic objective-seeking piecemeal reforms, and eventually the growth of a black middle class, while others saw the pact as a tactical move, intended to consolidate political gains and prepare for the next phase of the struggle. For imperialism, it was a tactical retreat intended to cut its losses, and to use economic statecraft to regain its monopoly position. This contestation was never fully resolved as the diverse elements among the security forces and their political parties sought control of the military apparatus and as South African destabilisation seriously unsettled the balance. This fuelled the Matabeleland conflict from 1982 to 1987, while the generalisation of the pact to Namibia and South Africa, raised false hopes for a regional peace and development dividend.

In the 1980s, Zimbabwe had been hailed as a model of political transition for the settler societies of Southern Africa, whereby majority rule was conditioned on property guarantees. It was also lauded for enhancing food security, despite the prevalence of food insecurity among 30 per cent of its population (Moyo 1986), and it was considered a pilot project for market-led land reform despite its failures to redistribute adequate land (Moyo 1995). Although white political privileges were phased out, Zimbabwe remained a racially divided society, in which the defence of 'human rights' served mainly to protect white property and race-based privilege. Neocolonialism in Zimbabwe, not only relegated the majority population to a permanent process of semi-proletarianisation and super-exploitation, it also constricted the emergence of a black middle class with roots of its own in the economy. The structural violence inherent in this 'post-white settler' type of neocolonialism (Mandaza 1985) was never pacified by piecemeal reforms, and when the country entered structural adjustment, even the visible social gains of the prior decade were reversed (Yeros 2002).

From a longer historical perspective, the accumulation needs of the petty-bourgeoisie could not be realised as the new neoliberal conditions of the 1990s created obstacles to accumulation and entrenched racial differentiation. The petty-bourgeoisie was soon forced back into a popular, inter-class black alliance against the *status quo* dominated by settler and foreign capital. The process was also fuelled by the social crisis (wage repression, retrenchments, etc) which generated greater labour militancy around 1995 and the escalation of scattered land occupations from 1996, reviving historic land movements (Moyo 2001). The sudden emergence of a political opposition backed by white farmers, capital, NGOs and western states, further entrenched the polarisation of land and electoral politics. Zimbabwe's liberal model was thus unravelled as expropriatory land reforms took hold thereafter (Moyo 2001).

At the time Zimbabwe's Fast Track Land Reform took off, a new wave of large-scale land and resource grabbing had been underway in Africa from the 1990s, especially in countries such as Mozambique and Zambia with land concentration and the privatisation of landed property creeping in, while the extroversion of agrarian production relations and markets persisted (Moyo 2008). This escalated in the mid-2000s, following a series of world-wide energy, food and financial crises. Under degenerating world-systemic conditions, the merchant path[2] of smaller scale and scattered land concentration, which had been emerging in the 1990s in non-settler Africa, was being overtaken by a wider process of large-scale land alienation led by foreign capital itself, often with domestic allies. This alienation is now installing a new 'junker' path[3] in non-settler Africa, as the accumulation trajectory rapidly evolves beyond the structures inherited at independence in the 1960s.

The African agrarian question is increasingly focused on the social questions of exclusion, inequality, food insecurity and poverty, resulting from growing land dispossession, the super-exploitation of labour and unequal trade and financial flows (Moyo, Tsikata and Diop 2013). Demands for popular sovereignty over land, minerals, oil and natural resources, now referred to as 'resource nationalism', place the political dimension of land rights ahead of the agrarian question of reversing 'backwardness' through industrial development. The politics of land is most explosive where the inequalities fuse class with race, nationality and ethnic differences, as well as with the gender inequities derived from the pervasive patriarchal order. Indeed, while the nascent domestic petty bourgoisie, in alliance with transnational capital and donors, is actively involved in the current land grabs, resistance to this process is a constant feature.

What makes Zimbabwe relatively unique or different now is that it has proposed new ways of deepening the transition to majority rule by means of radical land reform, and as happened elsewhere in Africa after decolonisation, through an 'indigenisation and empowerment' programme, focused on the mining sector. This has challenged the dominant neoliberal orthodoxy, ignited 'resource nationalism' to challenge Africa's potential 'recolonisation', and raised expectations for far-reaching land reforms in other former settler colonies.

Radicalised Land Reform Movement: Decentralised, Anti-Bureaucratic Alliance

The land movement was initiated by popular rural and urban mobilisation under the leadership of liberation war veterans, against the immediate policy of the ruling party and the state. The nationalist leadership stepped in during 1997, when it risked losing its most critical social bases, the peasantry and the war veterans, given that the latter permeated the security forces of the state apparatus. Its purpose was to control and co-opt the land movement, as well as to open a political space for the expression of pent up land demands among layers of the population, including many land occupations which were not directly organised by war veterans. Most crucially, the state accommodated the interests of the aspiring black bourgeoisie through a bifurcated land redistribution programme, providing for both peasant and small-scale capitalist farming. It also spared from redistribution certain farms owned by foreign capital, the state, and public trusts, ostensibly to maintain some critical food supplies and agro-industrial capacity, while promising to indigenise the foreign capital (Moyo 2010).

From the beginning, streamlining the land movement was critical to the state. It created District Land Committees in all the provinces, and supported the Committees of Seven on each farm, while diminishing the powers of local war veterans who were the vanguard of the land movement. In their place, civil servants, chiefs, and other war veterans, not connected directly to local struggles, were installed, thereby broadening and diluting the representation and class character of the land movement. Over the following years, gaining firm control over the movement was, however, made difficult by the war veterans' decentralised and anti-bureaucratic character, whose agency was enabled by historic and organic roots of social mobilisation developed during the armed struggle, and their encouragement of pre-existing localised land occupation movements. This structure of the land movement is the first distinctive feature underlying the success of this mass mobilisation,[4] unlike other representative organisations, including the formally constituted Zimbabwe National Liberation War Veterans Association (ZNLWVA). Unlike mass mobilisations elsewhere, in Zimbabwe, this decentralised structure was unified by the principle of radical nationalism.

The second distinctive characteristic of Zimbabwe's radicalisation was the extensive rural-urban spread of the land movement, in terms of active membership and physical participation in the land occupations. [5] The leadership of the land movement included local peasant leaders, local war veterans, spiritual leaders, some chiefs, and various working class activists, intellectuals, and political party leaders, in a cross-class alliance. Such local leaders played a vanguard role in galvanising the mobilisation of long-standing grievances over land and racial inequality. Political parties, farmers' unions, trade unions, and NGOs had not only lacked sufficient interest or organic roots in the land question, they were also structurally incapable of bridging the rural-urban gap in the interest of mass mobilisation. The land movement incorporated urban elements into rural land occupations and promoted land occupations in urban areas for residential purposes. This overcame the occupational corporatism of trade unions and farmers' unions, and the often divisive strategies of political parties, at a time when bureaucratic sclerosis and various sources of political polarisation had accentuated the rural-urban divide.

The ZCTU was eventually co-opted by foreign donors,[6] together with a broad array of liberal, urban-based, middle-class, donor-dependent NGOs, including the National Constitutional Assembly (NCA). By the time the ZCTU founded the Movement of Democratic Change (MDC) in 1999, the 'pro-democracy' forces had been completely overwhelmed by white-settler interests and foreign donors (see also Gwisai 2002). Black farmers' unions representing the peasantry had also during the 1990s, distanced themselves from the land reform agenda (Skalnes 1995), as petty-bourgeois interests prevailed among their ranks, focusing their advocacy on access to state subsidies and price-setting. Although they did not expressly oppose the land reform, they were unable to mobilise a constituency interested in repossessing land. On the other hand, the white-settler Commercial Farmers' Union (CFU), in alliance with GAPWUZ (the farm workers' trade union), mobilised both its membership and international public opinion against the land reform.

The relationship of the land movement to the nationalist leadership has posed conceptual difficulties since the ruling party, having succumbed to structural adjustment, changed course in the late 1990s towards a radical approach, while seeking to control the land movement. The 'pro-democracy' alliance, which claimed to be the vanguard of 'progressive' politics in Zimbabwe, sought credit for the ruling party's opting for a radical land reform programme (Raftopoulos 2009), as if there was no real political or historical basis for such radicalisation. With the mounting evidence of extensive land redistribution challenging neopatrimonialist claims of ethnicised elite capture, there is now a veiled acknowledgment of the vanguard role of the land movement. This role is however rendered as a mere component, together with the MDC alliance, of a broader 'passive revolution', that has 'remained largely under the control of the state', and putatively one that has 'largely politically marginalised the majority of the population' (Raftopoulos 2010:707). Such an interpretation obscures the distinctive features of a rare mass mobilisation, involving a range of forces which confronted the white agrarian monopoly and the imperialist alliance as a whole, to the effect of broadening the social base of the economy.

Part of the conceptual difficulties facing those who have opposed the petty-bourgeoisie outright arises largely because some political elites gained more than others through the A2 scheme. Masuko (2012) and Sadomba (2012) have argued that black capital never really broke ranks with monopoly capital and that it acted solely on the latter's behalf to control the land movement. Yet, the process of radicalisation integrated diverse class interests, including the petty-bourgeoisie and the semi-proletariat, against the white agrarian faction of monopoly capital. The breaking of ranks with monopoly capital is exemplified in the fact that the state redistributed over 5,000 properties, over and above the estimated 1,000 properties that were actually occupied by the land movement, and such acquisitions persisted beyond the immediate election contests (Moyo 2011a). While this radicalisation did not result in a socialist revolution, or in a generic 'passive revolution', the white agrarian establishment was essentially liquidated at farm level both economically and politically.

The role of the petty-bourgeoisie and the nationalist leadership, their use of the state, and their relationship with the movement can best be understood in terms of the character and function of the 'radicalised state'. By 2000, the state underwent a peculiar transformation, through a suspension of its bureaucratic coherence (its 'bureaucratism'), with many of its personnel mobilised in the interest of Fast Track Land Reform (Moyo and Yeros 2007a). The constitution of District Land Committees overrode local bureaucratic structures,[7] but it also established *fast-track* procedures and new capacities for the expropriation and redistribution of land, while also reforming laws and amending the constitution to underpin the action and defend land occupiers against eviction. One may rightly fault the ruling party for streamlining the land movement and creating space for the petty-bourgeoisie, but it is not the case that it fulfilled a reactionary role, for it did not defend the *status quo ante*. Contrary formulations do not adequately recognise the existence of *real* intra-class conflict, between petty-bourgeois and monopoly capital, black and white elites, and among black elites.

This suggests that Zimbabwe's radicalisation entailed another rare phenomenon of petty-bourgeois radicalism, shaped by pressures from the land movement, as well as by blatant external political interventions and sanctions. That the petty-bourgeoisie also became an agent of change presents very difficult political questions, as previous African scholars have noted (Fanon 1967; Shivji 1976). However, there is a problem in attributing radicalisation solely to certain local-level war veterans, against all the rest who vied for land, although the land movement did coalesce varied streams of land occupiers. Instead of one 'genuine' category of radicalism, there are different radicalisms, each with its own *class* project.

Others who claim to stand aloof of the difficult political questions have deployed a liberal-populist 'people *versus* state' dichotomy, rendering the whole land and agrarian reform process solely as a consequence of the agency of the landless against an indifferent state at best, or a 'commandist' and 'clientelist' state, at worst (see Scoones *et al.* 2010; Hanlon *et al.* 2013). Class analyses that reach similar conclusions do so only by downplaying the radicalisation of the petty-bourgeoisie and treating it as if it never really broke ranks with monopoly capital.

It would be more correct to say that the nationalist leadership in recent years had come to represent mainly *un-accommodated* bourgeois interests, which indeed have liberation convictions of their own, but which are under the illusion that they can reform monopoly capitalism so as to sustain a 'patriotic bourgeoisie' into the future. This situation explains the current scattered pressures for 'indigenisation' programmes in strategic industries, as opposed to more collectivist solutions (Moyo and Yeros 2011b, Moyo 2011b). It also partly explains the violence that accompanied land reform, mainly off the farms, as the nationalist leadership was unable to commit 'class suicide' and submit itself to the evolving and expanding popular demands on the ground (Moyo and Yeros 2009, 2011b). The bifurcation of the Fast Track Land Reform, the strategy of indigenising agro-estates and other industries, and the recurrent violence are manifestations, not only of class conflict, but also of *intra*-class conflict between petty-bourgeois interests and monopoly capital.

A related weakness may be attributed to the war veteran movement which became 'tactically sterile', and paid dearly for this when the state's Murambatsvina project assaulted urban settlements in 2005 (Sadomba 2013). An uninterrupted escalation of the revolutionary situation would have required that the land movement undergo organisational and ideological innovation founded in proletarian mobilisation and wider strategic concerns. Masuko (2013) argues that the land movement did go beyond the single-issue platform of land reclamation by promoting a plethora of associational forms that sprouted in the resettlement areas (see also Murisa 2013). While such associational forms are the kernel of progressive politics in the countryside, including their issue-focus on service provision by the state (agricultural inputs, social infrastructure, markets, credit, and subsidies), they are not articulated into a radical mass agrarian movement. This opportunity is dissipating, as the liberal 'pro-democracy' movement, comprising the donor-funded MDC, NGOs, and settler farmer elements, seek to mobilise such associations in service of a new market integration agenda.

The radicalised nationalist leadership could also be faulted for allowing other petty-bourgeois tendencies, since aspiring capitalists, lacking other means to bid for land, mobilised sub-national, ethno-regional claims to land 'rights' to exclude non-local competitors (Moyo 2011a). This tendency continues, and could escalate as land bidding is re-focused on the enlargement of existing landholdings at the expense of smallholders, and as bidding spreads to the redistribution of retained private and public agro-estates.

Such contradictions among the black petty-bourgeoisie could undermine its radical nationalist economic posture although these are essentially the ongoing tendencies of a class which remains profoundly insecure. Should the main 'enemy' come to be seen as 'internal' (including 'ethno-regional' or party political partisans), there could be regression to a neocolonial type of politics, malleable to foreign interests.[8] Yet, this is not a foregone conclusion " or a perennial and decontextualised 'ethnic' possibility in African politics" but reflects shifting strategies of accumulation, subject to pressures from above and from below. The re-grouping of popular forces is all the more necessary given the new tendencies of class formation at the top and the changing strategies of monopoly finance capital.

Structural Reform, Renewed Developmentalism and Economic Nationalism

The land reform radically restructured land ownership, but it did not 'oust capital', which itself is now re-grouping (Moyo 2011b). Instead, a broadly based tri-modal agrarian structure has been instituted, consisting of peasant, small-scale capitalist and large-scale estate farms (which are being indigenised). There was a deliberate promotion of competing trajectories of accumulation, mustered through the mediation of contradictory land struggles and class interests, and combined resistances to the opposition to reform by capital and Western donors. This outcome suggests another distinctive characteristic of the radicalisation process.

This agrarian structure is based on differential landownership regimes (state-sanctioned usufruct permits, non-tradable leases, and freehold or state property, respectively); different forms of integration into markets; varied forms of labour relations and varied linkages to non-farm activities and assets. This, in turn, gives rise to different types of producers vying for different forms of labour mobilisation and competing accumulation strategies (Moyo 2011b, 2011c). This has unravelled the legacy of the settler-colonial 'labour reserve' structures, by amplifying the smallholder sector and incorporating a significant 'merchant' path, while retaining elements (albeit downsized) of the 'junker' and 'state' paths (see Moyo and Yeros 2005a).[9] This has also restructured farm labour supplies and labour utilisation.

The diverse elements of this structure are not entirely unique to the continent, but their clear demarcation in state policy, and the dynamics by which they have been established, do make this case unique. Moreover, the reform brings Zimbabwe closer to the rest of Africa's agrarian structures by breaking up the large-scale farming established during the nineteenth-century, and broadening the small-scale capitalist sector, which had also been introduced by the colonial regime, while preserving some 'strategic' agro-industrial estates (Moyo 2011b).

The fundamental question is whether Zimbabwe will be able to sustain, via this tri-model structure, an introverted process of accumulation 'from below', given the tendencies and contradictions of this new agrarian structure, with regard to the new type of labour reserve that has emerged, incipient land markets, the persistence of the core agricultural exports and the re-insertion of finance capital through markets, credit and contracts. Moreover, the attendant processes of class formation and the contestations over accumulation and the policy regime, remain intrinsically fluid, given also the contradictions imposed by the extant sanctions regime.

For instance, one of the immediate consequences of Fast Track is the re-emergence of informal land rental markets between the 'better performers' and the 'weaker' ones, often between A2 and A1 farmers, respectively (Moyo *et al.* 2009). Both macroeconomic constraints and labour shortages, on both A1 and A2 farms, have contributed to this tendency. Land sharing is also common, although this often occurs among A1 farmers' kinship networks, as well as between all resettled farmers and farm workers, gold-panniers, and 'squatters' who have yet to be settled formally (Moyo *et al.* 2009). Such tendencies represent local class differentiation across all agro-ecological regions and heralds future conflicts over access to land and natural resources.

Although land tenure is generally seen to be secure, boundary and access disputes could intensify (Moyo 2013). One of the terrains of struggle that could intensify is the status of leasehold on A2 farms, which is being challenged by domestic and foreign elements which advocate the conversion of the current leasehold land rights into freehold tenures. In this case, small-scale capitalist farmers would find allies in private banks, which typically justify their refusal to finance resettlement farmers on the supposed absence of 'collateral'. Another terrain of struggle is the land tenure status of the remaining farm workers, some of whom have been re-inserted into labour-tenancy relations (Chambati 2013). Yet, state policy still remains committed to both leasehold tenure and the protection of farm workers against eviction from A2 lands.

Re-peasantisation and the break-up of the settler agrarian monopoly has diminished the labour reserve of the past and undermined the functioning of the colonial cheap-labour system. By 1999, half of this labour-force consisted of non-permanent, casual labour, reproducing itself precariously between the LSCF and the Communal Areas, on real farm wages which had collapsed to 24 per cent of the Poverty Datum Line. Super-exploitation was facilitated by a racialised, quasi-feudal labour-tenancy system, together with a patriarchal system of customary authority, which continued to undermine the bargaining power of the semi-proletariat as a whole (Moyo and Yeros 2005).

Land reform has absorbed surplus labour into petty-commodity production for own consumption and the market, and pried open access to natural resources and related land use values that previously were enclosed in the properties monopolised by white farmers (see also Chambati 2011). The immediate manifestation of this has been a shortage of labour, which has deprived especially the small-scale capitalist sector of the prior abundant workforce willing to work for wages below the cost of social reproduction.

That the labour reserve diminished and the bargaining power of labour altered does not, of course, mean that the labour reserve economy has been extinguished. The persistence of simple reproduction among smallholders and the reconstitution of the small- and large-scale capitalist sectors, under the weight of Western sanctions, continue to re-create the structural conditions of super-exploitation, even among the new self-exploited peasantry. Super-exploitation is further abetted by residual labour-tenancy on some new farms, as well as the exploitative intra-family and gender-based labour relations. Yet, the unravelling of racialised relations of personal dependence and the expansion of the smallholder sector has altered the balance of power among the three modes of farming. It is here that the new political struggle is now being fought.

State Interventionism, Indigenisation and New Developmentalism

Both small- and large-scale capitalist farmers have a structural interest in policy measures that will oblige small producers to work for wages below the cost of social reproduction. This interest would be reinforced should an export-oriented accumulation strategy predominate. But these two types of farmers are not identical, given that small-scale capitalist farmers, many with significant resource vulnerabilities, may also be co-opted by the state into production for domestic markets and industries. In fact, this objective has largely been their principal orientation to date. At the same time, smallholder farmers will themselves undergo differentiation, thereby adding to the labour pool. Yet, this may also be mitigated by inward-looking policy measures that both reinforce the conditions of smallholder production and induce the growth of cooperativism and rural industries capable of re-organising the labour process.

The political struggle between the three modes of farming and the attendant disputes over labour remain imbalanced and will be determined by a number of factors, including the character of state interventions against monopoly capital.

The dominant factor in shaping the accumulation trajectory is, however the structural power of monopoly capital, which opposed the radicalisation process and undermined progressive agrarian change by imposing severe limits on Zimbabwe's economic recovery. From the beginning of the Fast Track, financial isolation and a capital strike had led to a severe shortage in the economy, leading the state towards an interventionist economic strategy, initially without a comprehensive plan to defend against sanctions (Moyo and Yeros 2007a). A plan emerged as the internal and external contradictions escalated, although the key constraint was how to finance the plan. This interventionism under contemporary neoliberalism is the fifth distinctive characteristic of the Zimbabwe model.

It entailed controls over prices, trade, capital, and agricultural markets, the monopolisation of grain purchases by the Grain Marketing Board, and the setting of food production targets, as well as targeted subsidies to agriculture and industries, to bolster an erstwhile import substitution industrialisation. State-owned agro-estates, together with state interests in mining, banking, and other firms led this strategy, which includes the production of local agro-fuels against a rising fuel-import bill. An agricultural mechanisation policy sought to enhance motorised draught power, although the bulk of this was allocated to small- and large-scale capitalist farmers to compensate for the labour shortages that emerged (Moyo 2011a; Moyo and Nyoni 2013). State subsidies in electricity, fuel and transport facilities were also effected, albeit at low levels associated with the fiscal constraints. This plan reflected both the class bias of the state and its reaction to the generalised strike by private banks and, bilateral and multilateral donors.

Eventually, hyperinflation, political conflict and informalisation of economic activity compelled the state to attempt normalisation with international capital. It is through this process that the state 'interrupted' the momentum of the revolutionary situation, including the assault on urban land movements in 2005 to establish 'order' (Moyo and Yeros 2007a, 2009, 2011b). Indeed, the heterodox plan lacked the foresight to defend against the ensuing capital strike, which could have been better resisted by a policy of immediate nationalisation of banks and strategic industries. Thus, the state became susceptible to carrot-and-stick strategies by foreign capital, leading to its refusal to fully default on debt.

Normalisation has led to cooptation back towards an extroverted strategy through various mechanisms (Moyo 2011a, 2011b). The land redistribution policy on agro-estates is essentially a comprador 'indigenisation' strategy, which enables black capitalists to become majority shareholders in agro-estates, thereby succumbing to the logic of plantation agriculture and its associated financial circuit. The expansion of outgrower contract farming, linked to a similar external financial circuits, locks small-scale capitalists into the agro-estates for the production of sugarcane for the European market (under the ACP-EU Lomé Convention). So do the tobacco and cotton contracts tied to Chinese and Western capital.

Dependence on external finance, inputs, and markets has exercised overriding power in tilting, once again, the internal balance between social classes, while Western sanctions against Zimbabwe, including those against the parastatals spearheading the economic recovery, reinforce this. The adoption in 2008, at the peak of hyperinflation, of a neoliberal policy on currency, 'dollarisation' capital, trade, and agricultural markets may have been a tactical retreat, but it entrenches the cooptation.

Nonetheless, counter-tendencies suggest that the policy of normalisation has not totally extinguished the dirigisme of the state and the new black bourgeoisie, which is still acutely vulnerable to a monopolistic world market, and remains in conflict with international capital. The popular classes, from which the nationalist leadership must still claim legitimacy, are even more vulnerable. The state has not abandoned the ISI policy, or its intention to mediate pro-actively in favour of black capital and, secondarily the smallholder farmers. The Zimbabwean state persists with its policy of building national food self-sufficiency and to substitute for imported petrol by expanding the cultivation of sugarcane on agro-estates owned by the state and public trusts to produce ethanol for domestic transport, may have various local industrial spin-offs (Moyo 2011b). Such investments include via joint ventures with foreign capital, from the East, West, and South, under the 'Look East Policy' (LEP) inaugurated in 2004.

The class character of state power, the strategies of the black bourgeoisie, and the re-grouping of social forces are the three further factors that will co-determine the balance of forces, as suggested by the escalation of the indigenisation strategy beyond agriculture to secondary industries, banking, and mining. Generally, indigenisation is a multi-class strategy, whose class character has oscillated in accordance with the correlation of forces as the policy regime shifted.

In the 1980s, it shifted from a popular land reform policy to one geared towards the creation of a black bourgeoisie via affirmative action with respect to land and state commerce. The former continued throughout the 1990s, under structural adjustment, without much success, until its radicalisation during the Fast Track Land Reform Programme. Then, under the subsequent normalisation from 2005, the strategy shifted back to a bourgeois strategy, geared towards creating majority shareholding for black capitalists. Yet, a further elaboration of the policy from 2010 envisions joint ventures between state-owned enterprises and foreign firms. This policy is increasingly reflected in the mining sector (e.g. diamonds), which has enormous potential to fill foreign-exchange gaps.

Upon the discovery of massive diamond deposits, a struggle ensued, especially from 2007 onwards, for the control of the industry, against both small miners who entered the fray, as well as corporate capital of South African and Western origin. The strategy on diamonds, and the possibility of circumventing sanctions, led to a confrontation with foreign capital and small miners, and this entailed repression of the latter. In the event, the West, ostensibly in solidarity with the repressed small miners, resolved to broaden its sanctions tactics by invoking the 'Kimberly Certification Process', alleging these were 'conflict diamonds'. When Zimbabwe won Kimberly certification, the United States unilaterally imposed sanctions on the diamond mining firms in partnership with mining parastatals.

Nonetheless, state policy on minerals seems to be stabilising and is positioning the state to reap future profits, via joint ventures looking both East and West. The accommodation of Chinese capital has been central to this strategy. Similarly, the expansion of platinum production by Western multinationals was compelled by the threat of losing concessions to the East. Meanwhile, high-ranking state personnel have positioned themselves in the state-owned Zimbabwe Mining Development Corporation driving the joint ventures, which has undermined the legitimacy and transparency of the strategy.[10]

It is notable that the indigenisation policy has been elaborated, beyond the re-distribution of majority shareholding and joint ventures, towards a higher degree of social access, in the wake of popular agitation. This transformation involves the imposition of conditions on foreign firms to undertake investments in physical and social infrastructure, such as roads, schools, and clinics, as well as the allocation of shares to 'community and employee trusts'. The strategy reflects a renewed attempt, in response to more general criticisms of class bias, to broaden the benefits of indigenisation, especially of mining, to the rural areas. It also reflects the continued need of political elites (combining both ZANU-PF and MDC leaders) to respond to the reaction by capital, and to meet popular demands for state support in light of forthcoming elections.

Overall, these policies reflect the persistence of a specifically *nationalist* accumulation strategy promoted by black capitalists with connections to the state. For, despite having sunk roots of their own in the means of production, they remain vulnerable to both monopolistic forces and the need to maintain legitimacy *vis-à-vis* popular forces. Black capital continues to seek to consolidate its position by recourse to a pro-active state, against what it considers to be its main obstacle: Western monopoly capital.

New Agrarian Movements: Rural Cooperativism and Democratisation?

The sustainability of the current outcomes, and the potentials for further progressive reforms, will depend on the politics of the popular classes after land reform. While the larger farmers have been gravitating towards production for export markets (albeit still in minority numbers), the basic pillar of food sovereignty will remain the smallholder farmers, together with a significant portion of small-scale capitalists, who, for instance, dominate the rapid recovery of tobacco production. There has been a clear shift in the orientation of production towards food grains and pulses, to which the new land beneficiaries have dedicated 78 per cent of their cropped land. And, while national maize yields per hectare have suffered severe setbacks under conditions of drought, expensive inputs and sanctions, beneficiaries in wetter agro-ecological regions have performed much better (Moyo 2011c).

But the economic potential remains enormous, considering that land utilisation rates are already at 40 per cent « that is, the land utilisation level of the extroverted LSCF sector prior to Fast Track. But notable in this regard is that, on average, the A2 farmers with larger landholdings crop below 20 per cent of their land, while a few surpass the 50 per cent mark. In the absence of broad-based investments in infrastructure, fertiliser, and machinery due to credits supply constraints, fulfilment of the agricultural potential will be delayed. Furthermore, differentiation across class and regions will deepen, with adverse consequences for national cohesion and the weak rural movements. The emerging struggles over production, land access, tenure, and labour, as well as over the much-needed social services in general, require organised social forces capable of tilting the balance towards smallholders and farm workers (Moyo 2011c).

The most promising development is the emergence among 40 per cent of small producers of new local cooperative movements to pool labour, savings, and infrastructure, procure seeds and fertilisers, channel extension services, bid for producer prices, and negotiate labour contracts (Murisa 2012). Among the farm workers, there are group negotiations for access to land and improved conditions of work, although their poor representation by the national agricultural labour union (GAPWUZ), which has never been in favour of agrarian reform (Chambati 2013), is notable. Some of the farmer groups are orchestrated by state extension agents and private contract farming firms, while others are led by the war veteran groups. Yet others draw on kinship relations and existing former farming associations in the Communal Areas (see Murisa 2012).

De facto, the state had extended customary authority to resettlement areas, both as a cooptation tactic and a low-cost dispute-resolution mechanism, but the new constitution of 2013 limits their authority to Communal Areas. The state also co-opted chiefs through their inclusion into the A2 farming scheme and mechanisation, but it excluded chiefs from exercising real authority over A1 land permits and A2 leases. It has also maintained their subordination (in some power relations) to elected authorities in local government. Meanwhile, their cooptation into a new class position, where this has occurred, raises new questions regarding the trajectory of this institution, notwithstanding the ethno-regional structure of Fast Track having extended the kinship basis of customary authority. It has nonetheless been observed that beneficiaries from non-contiguous areas have not always embraced their new chiefs (Murisa 2012).

Rural cooperativism also holds the unique potential to transform gender relations and customary authority, to defend land rights and progressive agrarian change, as such, authority was the social and political pillar of historic super-exploitation, particularly of women. Fast Track Land Reform tripled the proportion of rural women holding land in their own right, yet women remain greatly under-represented (with below 20 per cent of all farm units). The land movement also opened political space for women, which was filled in mass numbers. Women however seldom held leadership positions in land committees and local farmer associations (see Murisa 2012). While new cooperativism is the most realistic vehicle for withering away the retrogressive patriarchal aspects of customary authority, there are class contradictions here too.

Quite critically, facing various agrarian demands from such organised groups and other influential actors, the state has remained interventionist since 2003. For instance, the state has also been active in supporting farmers' groups via agricultural extension officers, contrary to suggestions that new farmers have not received state support (*e.g.* Scoones *et al.* 2010; Cliffe *et al.* 2011) or that they have been re-tribalised (Worby 2003). The various measures which show that the small producers have thrived because of rather than lack of state support include: the protection of land occupiers, despite allowing some evictions to occur; the expanded role of marketing boards; trade protection; some subsidies to agro-industry and farmers (credit, inputs and machinery) before and after dollarisation; the ban on GMOs; and so forth.

Overall, it is clear that intervention into this fluid field by a new social agent based on cooperative and democratic principles can further erode customary authority, empower women, integrate farm workers and smallholders into agro-industrial production units, and expand the potential for the formation of alliances among cooperative producers nationwide. Such agency may fulfil the aspirations for popular agrarian change which are necessary after Fast Track, but this should go much further than welfarist measure to create efficient worker-controlled cooperatives to sustain the struggle against monopoly capitalism, and retain pressure on the reconfigured state.

These social dynamics may shape the future of rural and national politics, depending on the ability of rural cooperativism to deepen its scope and branch out to form wider political alliances. The resurrection of mass rural politics requires building up the new producer associations into an advanced, united, and autonomous cooperative movement of rural workers, capable, not only of obtaining *ad hoc* services, but also of dislocating the new black bourgeoisie from its political pedestal (Moyo and Yeros 2007a).

Concluding Remarks: Lessons from Zimbabwe

While the internal dynamics, including the class character of the land reform, the indigenisation strategy and ongoing social struggles will determine the ability of the state to sustain an inward-looking accumulation process and its legitimacy, the security context and the foreign policy have been crucial in creating the external conditions for sustaining the radical reform. In this context, despite Zimbabwe's relative geopolitical insignificance, the re-radicalisation of land reform has challenged outright the controlled character of the transitions to majority rule in settler-colonial Africa. For this reason, it has been characterised as an 'unusual and extraordinary threat' to the USA (President George Bush 2002), and subjected to a host of sanctions and isolation.

It is only the new SADC security framework which, despite all its prevarications, is anchored in a mutual defence pact that has effectively prevented the militarisation of the Zimbabwe question (Moyo and Yeros 2011b). Zimbabwe's Look East Policy is 'complementary, rather than [serving as] an alternative to engaging with the West' (Patel and Chan 2006:182) as it has neither turned its back on Western capital, nor accepted investment from China and the rest of the East or South without conditions. The LEP was pursued as a method of circumventing Western sanctions, while pressuring the West back into investing in Zimbabwe, on conditions consistent with its indigenisation and empowerment policy. This outcome raises wider questions about the external conditions which enable or undermine radical reform, particularly the nature of relations with neighbouring states.

Furthermore, while Zimbabwe has particularities of its own, the structural and social sources of radical change are firmly rooted in most societies of the Global South (see Moyo and Yeros 2005a, 2011a). This is not to say that radical change depends on mere 'will', and that political resignation should be answered by naïve voluntarism. The correlation of forces in every situation should be assessed, with the intention of changing it, not preserving it. This also means that a clear understanding of the state apparatus and state power must be developed. A blanket anti-statist policy of 'changing the world without taking power', which remains so hegemonic among social movements, ought to be replaced by a strategy and tactics which seek to alter state power and unravel the state apparatus in the interest of the oppressed; i.e. towards radical agrarian reform.

For mass mobilisations to endure the countervailing forces that will inevitably align against them, they must take seriously the agrarian component of society. The objective should not be merely to accumulate forces for change, but also to initiate a longer-term process of structural change and national resistance, of which the agrarian question is a fundamental component. All societies in recent years that have entered a process of radicalisation have discovered that their food dependence and their domestic disjuncture between agriculture, industry, and energy are crucial sources of vulnerability. This potential weakness means that mass mobilisation must also take seriously the project of 're-peasantisation' as an explicitly *modern* project, and as the only alternative in conquering autonomous development in the South (Amin 2012; Patnaik 2012).

The particular Zimbabwe experience suggests that redistributive land reform remains necessary to redress existing racial, social and spatial inequalities to advance socially inclusive agrarian societies and promote wider rural livelihoods, accommodating a diverse range of classes and ethno-regional entities, in the context of an innovative national development strategy. An African vision for agrarian change cannot be modelled around Eurocentric experiences of industrial transformation, which pretend to have arisen from a pacific evolution of economies of scale and a natural process of integration into the global neoliberal capitalist world based upon 'comparative advantage. This is neither a plausible nor feasible alternative. In countries such as South Africa and Namibia, what remains of the legacy of the Apartheid agrarian model is a deepening of class-race inequalities and the ongoing concentration of land ownership and capital, and social deprivation.

The challenges of broadly based agrarian transformation, in light of the uneven balance of forces require serious consideration, including more innovative state interventions that seek to promote a progressive accumulation trajectory, entailing new strategies of rural development. To prevent the persistent super-exploitation of wage labour and small producers in the context of globalised agrarian markets, the current weaknesses of small producer and market cooperatives will have to be addressed to countervail existing limited state agricultural protection and support. This requires both increased popular mobilisation and progressive reforms in the state.

Notes

1. The material in this speech was reworked from a chapter by Sam Moyo and Paris Yeros (2013): The Zimbabwe Model: Radicalisation, Reform and Resistance, *In* Moyo, Sam and W. Chambati (eds), The *Land and Agrarian Reform in Zimbabwe: Beyond White-Settler Capitalism,* Dakar: CODESRIA (2013).

2. A merchant path consist of non-rural capital, including merchant capital, petty bourgeois elements, bureaucrats, military personnel and professionals who gain access to land. They farm on a smaller scale than capitalist farms but are integrated into export markets and global agro-industry.

3. The junker path, formerly of landlords turned capitalists, has its variants in the white settler societies of Southern Africa, and it operates in tandem with transactional capital.

4. Formally constituted and bureaucratised organs of political representation, such as political parties, farmers' unions, trade unions, and NGOs failed to mobilise a radical land movement (see Moyo 2001; Yeros 2002; Moyo and Yeros 2005b).

5. Some contemporary parallels include Bolivia and, to a lesser degree, Venezuela (see Moyo and Yeros 2011a).

6. By 1995, trade unions, led by the Zimbabwe Congress of Trade Unions (ZCTU) had completely abandoned land reform as a political project (Yeros 2002).The ZCTU had

pried away from the control of the state in the late 1980s, and articulated a critique of structural adjustment in the early 1990s, but it gravitated towards a political project of 'good governance' and 'regime change', promoted by foreign donors and international trade unions.

7. Something that the 'chaos' theorists have seen as the 'destruction of the state' (Hammar *et al.* 2003)

8. The immediate manifestation of such a tendency would be the escalation of factional politics both within the ruling party and within the MDC (see Moyo and Yeros 2007b).

9. Class analysis of the new Zimbabwe must come to grips with the tendencies and contradictions of this tri-modal structure, and avoid theories of 'rentier economy' (Davies 2005) or 'crony capitalism' (Bond 2009), or notions of 'passive revolution', which are based on nebulous assessments of the new class relations (*e.g.* Raftopoulos 2010).

10. For some 'pro-democracy' forces (e.g. Cross 2011), this critique has become opportunistic, calling for the nationalisation of black capital but not Western capital!

References

Amin, S., 1972, 'Underdevelopment and Dependence in Black Africa: Origins and Contemporary Forms', *Journal of Modern African Studies*, Vol. 10, No. 4, pp. 503"24.

Amin, S., 2012, 'Contemporary Imperialism and the Agrarian Question', *Agrarian South: Journal of Political Economy*, Vol. 1, No. 1.

Bond, P., 2009, 'Mamdani on Zimbabwe Sets Back Civil Society', *ACAS Bulletin*, Vol. 82 (March). (http://concernedafricascholars.org/bulletin/82/bond).

Cross, E., 2011, 'Nationalise Zimbabwe's Diamond Mines', *Africa Legal Brief*, 8 October. (http://www.africalegalbrief.com/index.php/component/content/article/367-nationalise-zimbabwes-diamond-mines-eddie-cross.html).

Chambati, W., 2011, 'Restructuring of Agrarian Labour Relations after Fast Track Land Reform in Zimbabwe', *Journal of Peasant Studies*, Vol. 38, No. 5, pp. 1047"68.

Chambati, W., 2013, 'Changing agrarian labour relations after land reform in Zimbabwe', in S. Moyo and W. Chambati, eds., *Land and Agrarian Reform Zimbabwe: Beyond White-Settler Capitalism,* Dakar: CODESRIA, pp. 157-194.

Davies, R., 2005, 'Memories of Underdevelopment: A Personal Interpretation of Zimbabwe's Decline', in B. Raftopoulos and T. Savage, eds., *Zimbabwe: Injustice and Political Reconciliation*, Cape Town and Harare: IJR and Weaver Press.

Fanon, F., 1967, *The Wretched of the Earth*, trans. C. Farrington, London: Penguin Books.

Hammar, A., Raftopoulos, B. and Jensen, S., eds, 2003, *Zimbabwe's Unfinished Business: Rethinking Land, State and Nation in the Context of Crisis*, Harare: Weaver Press.

Hanlon, J., Manjengwa, J. and Smart, T., *'Zimbabwe Takes Back Its Land'*, Auckland Park: Kumarian Press.

Mandaza, I., 1985, 'The State and Politics in the Post-White Settler Colonial Situation', in Mandaza, I., ed., *Zimbabwe: The Political Economy of Transition, 1980"1986*, Dakar: CODESRIA.

Masuko, L., 2013, 'Nyabira-Mazowe War Veterans Association: A Microcosm of the National Land Occupation Movement', in Moyo, S. and Chambati, W., eds, *Land and Agrarian Reform Zimbabwe: Beyond White-Settler Capitalism*. Dakar, CODESRIA, pp. 123-156.

Matondi, P., 2012, *Zimbabwe's Fast Track Land Reform*. London: Zed Books.

Moyo, S., 1986, 'The Land Question', in Mandaza, I., ed., *Zimbabwe: The Political Economy of Transition, 1980-1986*, Dakar: CODESRIA.

Moyo, S., 1995, *The Land Question in Zimbabwe*, Harare: SAPES Books.

Moyo, S., 2000, *Land Reform under Structural Adjustment in Zimbabwe: Land Use Change in Mashonaland Provinces*, Uppsala: Nordic Africa Institute.

Moyo, S., 2001, 'The Land Occupation Movement and Democratisation in Zimbabwe: Contradictions of Neo-liberalism', *Millennium: Journal of International Studies*, Vol. 30, No. 2, pp. 311-330.

Moyo, S., 2008, *African Land Questions, Agrarian Transitions and the State: Contradictions of Neoliberal Land Reforms*, Dakar: CODESRIA.

Moyo, S., 2010, 'Rebuilding African Peasantries: Inalienability of Land Rights and Collective Food Sovereignty in Southern Africa', Mimeo.

Moyo, S., 2011a, 'Three Decades of Agrarian Reform in Zimbabwe', *Journal of Peasant Studies*, Vol. 38, No. 3, pp. 493-531.

Moyo, S., 2011b, 'Land Concentration and Accumulation after Redistributive Reform in Post-Settler Zimbabwe', *Review of African Political Economy*, Vol. 38, No. 128, pp. 257-276.

Moyo, S., 2011c, 'Changing Agrarian Relations after Redistributive Land Reform in Zimbabwe', *Journal of Peasant Studies*, Vol. 38, No. 5, pp. 939-966.

Moyo, S., 2013, 'Land Reform and Redistribution in Zimbabwe since 1980', in Moyo, S., and Chambati, W., eds, *Land and Agrarian Reform Zimbabwe: Beyond White-Settler Capitalism*, Dakar, CODESRIA, pp. 29-78.

Moyo, S. and Yeros, P., 2005a, 'The Resurgence of Rural Movements under Neoliberalism', in Moyo S. and Yeros, P., eds, *Reclaiming the Land: The Resurgence of Rural Movements in Africa, Asia and Latin America*, London and Cape Town: Zed Books and David Philip.

Moyo, S. and Yeros, P., 2005b, 'Land Occupations and Land Reform in Zimbabwe: Towards the National Democratic Revolution?', in Moyo S. and Yeros, P. eds, *Reclaiming the Land: The Resurgence of Rural Movements in Africa, Asia and Latin America*, London and Cape Town: Zed Books and David Philip.

Moyo, S. and Yeros, P., 2007a, 'The Radicalised State: Zimbabwe's Interrupted Revolution', *Review of African Political Economy*, Vol. 111: pp. 103-121.

Moyo, S. and Yeros, P., 2007b, 'The Zimbabwe Question and the Two Lefts', *Historical Materialism*, Vol. 15, No. 3: pp. 171-204.

Moyo, S. and Yeros, P., 2009, 'Zimbabwe Ten Years On: Results and Prospects', *MRzine*, 10 February. (http://mrzine.monthlyreview.org/2009/my100209.html).

Moyo, S. and Yeros, P., 2011a, 'The Fall and Rise of the National Question', in Moyo S. and Yeros, P., eds, *Reclaiming the Nation: The Return of the National Question in Africa, Asia and Latin America*, London: Pluto Press.

Moyo, S. and Yeros, P., 2011b, 'After Zimbabwe: State, Nation and Region in Africa', in Moyo, S. and Yeros, P., eds, *Reclaiming the Nation: The Return of the National Question in Africa, Asia and Latin America*, London: Pluto Press.

Moyo, S. and Nyoni, N., 2013, 'Changing Agrarian Relations after Redistributive Land Reform in Zimbabwe', in Moyo, S. and Chambati, W., eds., *Land and Agrarian Reform Zimbabwe:Beyond White-Settler Capitalism,* Dakar: CODESRIA, pp. 195-250.

Moyo, S. and Yeros, P., 2013, 'The Zimbabwe Model: Radicalisation, Reform and Resistance', in Moyo, S. and Chambati, W., eds, *Land and Agrarian Reform Zimbabwe :Beyond White-Settler Capitalism,* Dakar: CODESRIA, pp. 331-357.

Moyo, S., Tsikata, D. and Diop, Y., 2013, 'Africa's Diverse and Changing Land Questions', in *Land in the Struggle for Citizenship in Africa*, Dakar: CODESRIA (forthcoming).

Moyo, S., Yeros, P. and Jha, P., 2012, 'Imperialism and Primitive Accumulation: Notes on the New Scramble for Africa', *Agrarian South: Journal of Political Economy*, Vol. 1, No. 2, pp. 181-203.

Murisa, T., 2013, 'Social Organisation in the Aftermath of "Fast Track": An Analysis of Emerging Forms of Local Authority, Platforms of Mobilisation and Local Cooperation', in Moyo, S. and Chambati, W., eds, *Land and Agrarian Reform Zimbabwe: Beyond White-Settler Capitalism,* Dakar: CODESRIA, pp. 251-290.

Patel, H. and Chan, S., 2006, 'Zimbabwe's Foreign Policy: A Conversation', *The Round Table*, Vol. 95, No. 384, pp. 175-190.

Patnaik, P., 2012, 'The Peasant Question and Contemporary Capitalism: Some Reflections with Reference to India', *Agrarian South: Journal of Political Economy*, Vol. 1, No. 1.

Raftopoulos, B., 2009, 'The Crisis in Zimbabwe, 1998-2008', in Raftopoulos, B. and Mlambo, A.S., eds, *Becoming Zimbabwe: A History from the Pre-colonial Period to 2008*, Harare and Johannesburg: Weaver Press and Jacana Media.

Raftopoulos, B., 2010, 'The Global Political Agreement as a "Passive Revolution": Notes on Contemporary Politics in Zimbabwe', *The Round Table*, Vol. 99, No. 411, pp, 705"718.

Sadomba, W., 2013, 'A Decade of Zimbabwe's Land Revolution: The Politics of War Veterans Vanguard', in Moyo, S. and Chambati, W., eds, *Land and Agrarian Reform Zimbabwe: Beyond White-Settler Capitalism,* Dakar: CODESRIA, pp. 79-122.

Scoones, I., Marongwe, N. Mavedzenge, B. Mahenehene, J. Murimbarimba, F. and Sukume, C., 2010, *Zimbabwe's Land Reform: Myths and Realities*, Suffolk, Harare and Johannesburg: James Currey, Weaver Press and Jacana Media.

Shivji, I.G., 1976, *Class Struggles in Tanzania*, New York and London: Monthly Review Press.

Skalnes, T., 1995, *The Politics of Economic Reform in Zimbabwe: Continuity and Change in Development*, New York: St. Martin's Press.

USAID, 2012, Zimbabwe USAID-BEST Annexes. BEST Project Bellmon Estimation Studies for Title II (BEST). Fintrac Inc.

Worby, E., 2003, 'The End of Modernity in Zimbabwe? Passages from Development to Sovereignty', in Hammar, A., Raftopoulos, B. and Jensen, S., eds, *Zimbabwe's Unfinished Business: Rethinking Land, State and Nation in the Context of Crisis*. Harare: Weaver Press.

Yeros, P., 2002, *The Political Economy of Civilisation: Peasant-Workers in Zimbabwe and the Neo-Colonial World*, PhD Thesis, University of London.

4

Out of Africa: Aid versus Capital Flight

Jomo Kwame Sundaram

Since the past decade, it has been said that Africa has been experiencing an economic revival. Economically, Africa has started to grow again after a quarter of a century of stagnation, and this is said to be the new hope for the future. There is even talk about this being Africa's century. Two other recent developments are significant to us here.

The second important development is the financial crisis, which began in 2007 and 2008. Three organisations anticipated the crisis. The Bank of International Settlements in Switzerland, UNCTAD and the UN Secretariat were very concerned with some implications of financial liberalisation and globalisation. [The G24 is the caucus of developing countries in Washington at the Bretton Woods Institutions (the IMF and the World Bank). In early 2007, the G24 came out with a 'policy brief' warning about the implications and consequences of the US housing bubble bursting.] Now, of course, we are in a different phase of the crisis. Much of Europe is facing the prospect of protracted economic stagnation, with all that it entails. This opens new possibilities for reform not previously available, as more influential countries are suffering its consequences.

Third, we are now facing multiple challenges, including the likelihood of continued global warming and its implications for human existence and for nature. We need to be able to address these multiple challenges in coherent ways. We have a huge challenge, but also a major obligation to understand these developments.

But we are also faced with an absence of leadership again. With the failure of leadership in the 1930s to deal with the Great Depression, we saw the rise of fascism, of militarism, and eventually, the Second World War with its devastating consequences. And although this is not imminent at present, we have seen some very ugly developments in many parts of the world. Unfortunately, we do not see leadership for this coming from other parts of the world.

Let me proceed by recalling the recent past because we run the risk of making very serious mistakes if we do not learn from the past. First, recall the history of African economic development, particularly from the late 1970s until the early part of the last decade. In other words, economic stagnation was certainly not a permanent condition of Africa. In the 1960s and 1970s, during the first decade or so after decolonisation, Africa was actually doing much better than in preceding or subsequent years.

With independence coming later to Africa than to colonial Asia and, of course, Latin America, Africa was relatively late in embarking on industrialisation, in trying to promote rural development and so on. When the oil price increased during the 1970s, these early post-colonial development initiatives were undermined. Stagflation in the West also inhibited the continued development of Africa. Structural Adjustment Programmes (SAPs), introduced in Africa during the 1980s and 1990s, generally made things worse. Almost a thousand structural adjustment programmes were introduced in Africa. The consequent decline in per capita income in the continent during the first half of the 1990s was about 3 per cent on average.

The typical policy conditionalities imposed in Africa at that time are well known, sometimes comparable to what is happening in Europe now: cuts in public spending, restraints on public credit, and elimination of subsidies. All this resulted in a reduction of demand, incomes, output and, of course, economic stagnation. Sub-Saharan African trade balances certainly did not improve over this period, despite the heavy price that was paid. Incredibly, despite some critical rethinking at the World Bank in recent years, not least by the late Ghanaian Vice President Gobind Nankani and Chief Economist for Africa, John Page, the current Chief Economist for Africa is adamant that the SAPs paved the way for African growth in the last decade.

The debt which many African countries got into during this period rose very significantly, not unlike the debt which European countries have incurred during the last few years. In response to the financial crisis, they borrowed heavily in order to save their banking and financial systems. In Africa, then, the debt increased significantly and became a huge albatross around the neck of Africa, stifling its ability to grow and develop.

Africa has become reliant on primary commodity production and commodity prices as a consequence. It is important to recall that the last century has seen a progressive decline in the prices of primary commodities, particularly through the 1980s and 1990s, which continued until the middle of the last decade. This decline has been reversed with very mixed consequences in the recent decade. But African terms of trade have been worse than the general decline referred to earlier. Caribbean economist W. A. Lewis pointed out, many years ago, that for a number of reasons, including the far lower subsistence levels in poor tropical countries, tropical agricultural prices have been much lower than for their temperate agriculture counterparts. As a consequence, tropical agriculture has been doing generally worse than temperate agriculture in terms of the prices of their respective agricultural products. As a consequence, the terms of trade of Africa – as an exemplar of tropical agricultural production – have generally developed much more unfavourably. To make matters worse, mineral prices also declined, especially after the second oil price hike at the end of the 1970s.

Recently, of course, mineral prices have gone up. Agriculture prices have also gone up, but certainly not to the levels of the 1970s, for example. But mineral prices, especially for some minerals, have gone up very high. Countries heavily dependent on resource extraction, particularly mineral extraction, are particularly vulnerable to the vagaries of prices. It is very important to remember that in many mineral extraction processes, relatively few workers are employed.

Despite Africa's transformation as the consequence of trade liberalisation, it is very important to recognise that Africa's share of world trade has actually declined. Recently, there is greater trade within Africa as well as greater trade with Asia, particularly with China and India. This is partly due to the growth of a particular type of South-South trade.

African reliance on primary commodity exports is generally high, with some countries being much more dependent than others. Most African countries depend heavily on primary exports but the degree of value addition, in the sense of processing primary commodities, is generally low. Among primary commodity exports, the mineral content is especially high. African agriculture has not really progressed very much during this period despite all the promises about the benefits of trade liberalisation and other types of economic liberalisation. So, greater reliance on mineral exports has been mainly responsible for recent growth.

For many countries, the degree of reliance on a few export commodities has also gone up. Export concentration has also gone up, with little diversification of Africa's exports. Of course, when you find a major new valuable mineral, let us say petroleum or gold, there will be a significant increase in output and exports. But, there has not been significant diversification in terms of the range of exports.

The great hope for Africa is still supposed to be agricultural trade liberalisation. It is claimed that if you open up agricultural markets, Africa will gain. Unfortunately, the net gains for sub-Saharan Africa are acknowledged to be negative, even by proponents of these arguments, e.g. see the studies by the World Bank published in 2005. There is no evidence whatsoever that there will be a significant increase in net African agricultural exports.

Agriculture's share of sub-Saharan African exports (except for South Africa) declined from the second half of the 1990s from about 28 per cent to about 18 per cent during the first half of the past decade. Developing countries, particularly African countries, have been told: 'don't worry about food security in the new international division of labour. As long as you produce and export, you can meet your import requirements, you can import your food, and so on. Leave it to the more efficient food producers to produce food'. As a consequence of such claims, Africa was transformed from a net food exporter during the 1980s into a net food importer in the last decade. Ironically, the African middle class benefits from the subsidies for European food production. If European food was not subsidised, the prices for imported food in Africa would probably be higher. Of course, Africans can significantly increase food production. But the new non-African interest in investing in food production in Ethiopia, Tanzania and other African countries is not necessarily going to feed more Africans.

It is very possible that if these investments succeed, Africa will no longer be a net food importer, as it is now. It will become a net food exporter again, but this does not necessarily mean that Africa will be better off in terms of food security. It does not mean that Africans will be better off because the continent is exporting more food. This is the tragedy and irony of the present situation. This basically underscores that African trade liberalisation is not good for sub-Saharan Africa (Table 1). The 'welfare-gains' from food merchandise trade liberalisation for sub-Saharan Africa are modest. The combination of agricultural trade liberalisation for developing countries, including Africa, plus agricultural subsidies in Europe, Japan and North America, has resulted in greater food insecurity.

Table 1: Projected welfare gains
from full merchandise trade liberalisation

	Total Welfare Gains	Gains from Developed Countries' Liberalization	Gains from Developing Countries' Liberalization	Agric., Food + Other Primary	Manu-factures
Global	254.3	139.6	114.7	167.51	86.8
Developed	146.2	96.6	49.6	121.84	24.4
Economies in transition	6.4	4.5	1.9	3.51	2.9
SSA	4.6	2.6	2.0	3.95	0.6
Middle East + North Africa	0.3	-1.0	1.2	-3.15	3.4
Latin America	35.7	17.9	17.8	23.03	12.7
Asian NICs + China	22.3	5.1	17.2	1.62	20.7
South Asia	15.4	9.0	6.4	5.72	9.7
Rest of world	23.4	4.9	18.5	10.99	12.4

Source: Anderson, Martin and van der Mensbrugghe, World Bank, 2005.

Another consequence of trade liberalisation has been the de-industrialisation of Africa. Ghana got its independence in 1957, and other countries later, with the Portuguese colonies last, in 1975. As noted earlier, decolonisation came much later in Africa compared to Asia and, of course, Latin America. So, the opportunity and time for import substituting industries to begin to emerge was much less. As a consequence, African industry is very limited as it was exposed to intense trade liberalisation and competition. The consequence, of course, has been that the share of manufacturing in national income in many African countries, including South Africa, has declined. Thus, the modest African industrialisation during the 1960s and the 1970s has been reversed since the 1980s.

There are many things which trade negotiators need to look at, including the bias in the system of tariffs. Western tariff structures discriminate against most developing countries and, arguably, against Africa in particular. So, the preferential trade arguments offered to Africans – sometimes to divide Africa from other developing countries, or to divide African LDCs from other LDCs – are often double-edged swords. Something is given with one hand, and something else taken with the other. Furthermore, general trade liberalisation within a multi-lateral system has significantly eroded what little advantage there was under the preferential trade agreements, which will adversely affect prospects for African industrialisation as well.

For Africa, the adverse consequences of trade liberalisation have been significant. But at the global level, financial globalisation has actually been far more important. Many countries in Africa aspire to be integrated into the international financial system. They often aspire to become 'emerging markets', thinking that they will be significantly better off.

But one consequence of international financial liberalisation or financial globalisation has been what is called 'capital account liberalisation'. The claim is that if you open the capital account, capital will flow from the capital rich countries to the capital poor ones. Even relatively conservative economists like Nobel laureate Robert Lucas has noted that capital has been flowing in the opposite direction – the so-called 'Lucas paradox'. He described this as capital flowing uphill. Thus, when you open the capital account, capital flows out, instead of coming in. Very often, it flows out through borrowing from abroad — the government borrows from abroad while private capital goes out. That has been happening in recent decades. This has been quite devastating and has many adverse consequences as well. Much of the other financial flows into Africa have also not contributed to the economic development of Africa, e.g. see the new book by the former chief economist at the African Development Bank, Leonce Ndikumana and his Amherst colleague James Boyce (see Map 1). Basically, flows from Africa are quite significant, especially growing during the past decade. [As Nigeria is a very important oil producer and exporter, it is exceptional]. There have been tremendous outflows of capital from sub-Saharan Africa. So, despite the impression of significant net flows to sub-Saharan Africa, 40 per cent of private Africa wealth was invested outside Africa some years ago. There is little reason to believe that the situation has significantly improved in recent years.

Capital flight has been very significant worth much of this facilitated by debt flows. While net capital flight is often responsive to conditions, but the net trend is clear. African debt repayments, including debt service payments, exceed debt receipts. And this has led to very significant outflows of financial resources from Africa.

Map 1: Cumulative Capital Flight from Sub-Saharan Africa, 1970-2008

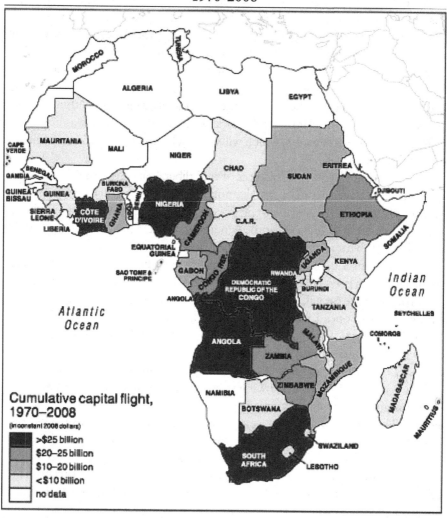

Source: Ndikumana and Boyce, 2011.

The Busan (Korea) November 2011 conference organised by the OECD Development Assistance Committee (DAC) has shifted its focus from aid to development effectiveness. Instead of looking at aid flows, we need to focus on net transfers. For the DRC in 2003, for example, there was an inflow of US$5.4 billion, but US$5 billion left in other forms, for various payments. So, the actual inflow to the DRC was only US$400 million. So, careful book keeping is very important to understand this phenomenon. What we really have, unfortunately, are huge transfers *out of Africa* – to use the title of a famous novel.

There are other reasons to be wary of financial liberalisation. First, there are relatively few so-called emerging market economies in Africa. Part of the reason is it takes a lot to do everything required to be recognised as an emerging market. The costs are very high and your problems are not necessarily over just because you have become recognised as an emerging market economy. You automatically have a new set of problems to deal with due, for example, to the 'credit rating' system which is biased. This means very few African countries can expect to get an AAA rating to begin with. But even getting an A rating or AB rating, constrains the government, especially the finance ministry and the central bank, from doing anything developmental which might be rejected by the market.

This is no longer just an African problem as we look at what has been happening in Europe recently. Part of the problem is having leaders who are looking over their shoulders at market signals all the time. They are unable to make decisions because they are always worrying over what the market would say. So, you have leaders held hostage by the 'invisible hand' of the bond market. Here, we are basically surrendering to an unaccountable invisible hand with the ability to inflict great damage.

Now, financial liberalisation is not inherently developmental by any stretch of the imagination. Most importantly, financial liberalisation causes financial institutions and markets to become more pro-cyclical. So, when you need the macroeconomic capacity to mitigate or ameliorate the ups and downs of markets, you lose that capacity because you have to behave in a pro-cyclical way to be considered market-friendly – which is what governments and authorities are compelled to do with this kind of liberalisation.

Basically, financial liberalisation tends to depress macroeconomic impact, and not only in Africa. Financial liberalisation also destroys development banks and financial institutions. In recent decades, they have been asked to conform to the rules of the game for commercial banks. Thus, the ability of development banks to provide long-term financing for development is undermined. Various initiatives to develop inclusive financial institutions have also been undermined by financial liberalisation. Africa only attracts about 2 per cent of total global FDI. To be able to attract FDI, governments often pursue policies which reduce possible gains from the FDI; hence, the actual gains from FDI are really quite modest.

For example, Tanzania has recently emerged as the third largest gold producer in Africa, after South Africa and Ghana. Guess how much Tanzania gains from gold mining in Africa? The answer is negative. Tanzania actually subsidises foreign gold mining companies. The reason: advice from an international financial institution that it should stimulate gold mining with tax breaks, infrastructure and other incentives for gold mining companies to invest in Tanzania.

Hence, all the transparency possible will not necessarily ensure that a country will be better off. Better transparency may reduce some types of corruption, but development will not necessarily follow. Meanwhile, many African countries have actually achieved greater macro-economic stability by various criteria, but again, development has not necessarily followed.

Figure 1: FDI Flows by Region, 2011

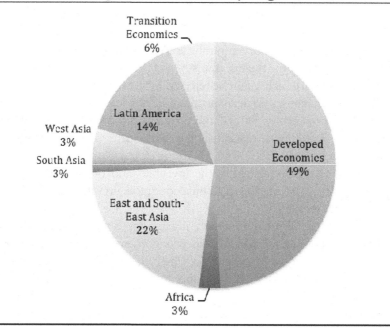

Figure 1 shows how small Africa's share of global FDI is, despite much FDI inflow into SSA mineral and other natural resource extraction. Generally speaking, there have been much higher returns to FDI in Africa than in any other region of the world. Unfortunately, the beggar-thy-neighbour competition among host governments trying to offer more attractive incentives to prospective investors reduces the net benefits. That was what happened in the Tanzanian gold mining, for example. As a result, certain countries considered 'FDI darlings' may attract more FDI, resulting in greater investment and growth, but at the expense of net development gains.

Much has been said in the last decade about the development potential of remittances. Remittances are supposed to boost development in Africa, especially if the *marabout* of Senegal can organise a better *hawala* system to bring back more money. This could help. Unfortunately, with the crisis in recent years, the adverse situation, particularly in the West, has reduced the ability of emigrants to remit money home.

In Figure 2, one can hardly see the third bar for ODA to Africa of US$26 billion in 2009. In contrast, the G20 countries' recovery efforts cost close to US$20 trillion in 2009; this gives a sense of the money available and the funds going to Africa. Of course, there are other considerations in discussing ODA. As you know, Dambisa Moyo's book is correctly critical of aid to Africa. However, if you leave out the most politicised aid – to Afghanistan, Iraq, Israel, Egypt and Colombia – the data suggests a modest positive effect of aid on growth, though of course, there is much room for improvement. But in the present economic situation, the likelihood of the Gleneagles aid commitments to Africa being met in the near future is probably bleaker than ever. ODA commitments in many countries often tend to be the first to be cut with fiscal austerity, which is likely to continue in much of the West for some years to come.

Figure 2: G-20 Recovery Effort vs. ODA to Africa USUS$ billions

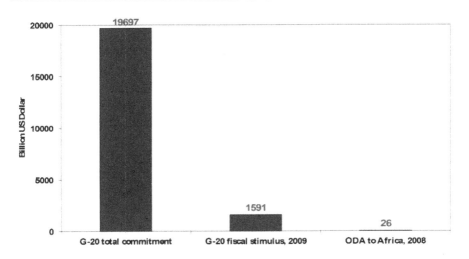

I hope I have conveyed an understanding of the current challenges and also of available opportunities. Ironically, much of Europe is now experiencing some of the problems which caused African stagnation for a quarter of a century. Perhaps, coming out of an emerging mutual appreciation of common problems, we have the possibility of changing some things at the international level in order to create a friendlier international environment, both on the trade and financial fronts, which will be much more development-friendly, particularly for Africa. For example, in light of common fiscal constraints, there may finally be greater willingness to cooperate internationally to enhance tax revenues for all, instead of continuing the 'beggar-thy-neighbour' tax competition, resulting in a 'race to the bottom'.

5

Let My Work Not Be in Vain: Doing Matriarchy, Thinking 'Matriarchitarian' with Africa in the Twenty-first Century

Ifi Amadiume

With protests and movements everywhere cutting through the gloom and doom of failed economics, suddenly there is a promising and inspirational atmosphere in which to think, write and agitate for good progress and useful change. It is particularly heartening to see the youth again involved in a popular movement that articulates a collective, participatory alternative in ideals of equity and justice!

It is good to see that anti-capitalist movements are about criticising social inequality, demanding participatory inclusiveness and fighting for social, economic and political justice. Much of our work on this topic have revolved around the relationship between the state and civil society, mostly from a class and gender perspective, and to the exclusion of indigenous and first peoples rights, except perhaps in peasant studies that are markets or modes of production related. The upsurge of the environmental movement, climate change concerns, protests and negotiations, as many now recognise as possible sources of anti-capitalism and alternative development ideas and practices, call for broader methodological and theoretical perspectives to meet new challenges and take on difficult questions.

The above is what is implied in the title of this address, which is in recognition of the legacy of Cheikh Anta Diop and the importance of his work for Africa and the challenges of the 21st century and beyond. One is the legacy of self-directed historical achievements that Africa brings to a comparative global perspective on our knowledge of world civilisations. The other is about the generating of working ideas and principles that Africa can apply locally in a comparative way for Africa's own development. Years of working with Igbo empirical data and developing a theory of gender based on a matriarchal paradigm have enabled me to see the importance of a matriarchal perspective both in the local and in an African and international global reality. I want to apply this perspective in a pan-Africanist way that argues that a matriarchal tradition presents a counter-hegemonic alternative to a colonially inherited patriarchal dominance, as it generates and supports women's leadership and enables the expression of a more flexible gender identity. I will use illustrative examples from West Africa, the Nile Valley and South Africa.

Our usual civil society bias in the study of women's rights and social justice is partly responsible for the marginalisation of indigenous communities and cultures. The use of terms such as traditional or traditions (that I employ regardless) becomes problematic and is seen as retrogressive and condoning backward customs. Yet, there is no substitute for these terms in dealing with marginalised African geographies and societies where the majority of Africans live and produce culture. There is also a top-down economic-speak bias that marginalises the economic production of these communities. Thus, it is not surprising that great historical achievements of African women's matriarchy is not made an important basis of contemporary social and political configurations, both in scholarship and social practice.

Igbo societies, such as Nnobi, present a wealth of history and knowledge about matriarchal achievements and women's input in all aspects of social production and relations. Nnobi presents a useful study of what I might describe as saturated leadership; some might understand this as integrated leadership, while others might also see it as participatory leadership. What is it that enables this saturated integration of women's leadership into the social, economic and political structures of this society that we do not see in the colonially imposed modern society and state? They are daughters of gods and goddesses. Women also generate narratives and philosophies that are part of the paradigmatic conversation and contestation of social principles of matriarchy and, indeed, patriarchy as well. There are parallel men's and women's organisations at every level of the social structure, each with its leadership at every level.

Thus, the combination of organisation, presence in economic production and markets, including self-reflection in religion and rituals, all combine to accentuate the important role and achievements of "women in traditional settings throughout pre-colonial African history". In many cases women are able to translate economic importance or success into ritually acknowledged political power; ritual authority also brings recognised social and political power.

Like Igbo women, their neighbouring women of the Niger Delta are equally organised, and are producers of culture. I have proposed also teaching an awareness of the environmental pollution and the degradation of places like the Niger Delta by oil companies through knowledge of the cultural and traditional ritual ceremonies of the local communities that demonstrate the beauty and holistic relationship between women's creative imagination and their stunning body art and symbolisms, all merging, blending and holistically harmonising with their natural environment in a sustaining, renewable mutuality.

Africa has a deep history of women as cultural producers and leaders that stretches across the continent. We should remind ourselves of the wide geographical distribution of accounts of women leaders "of pre-colonial and traditional Africa" and women's expressions of rituals of political authority in the different political systems and societies in African history. We have women leaders, healers and economic producers in small nomadic band systems of the hunting and gathering societies, as for example, the Mbuti, Ndembu, San, etc. There are the women's cultural systems in the decentralised descent-based agricultural or pastoral societies, for example, the Igbo and Wadaabe. Women leaders are at the head of centralised political systems and feature in descent systems at the base, like the old chiefdoms of the Lovedu, Ashanti, Igbo.

Women leaders abound much deeper in African antiquity and in the ancient empires. A few West African examples of such women leaders at the top are Queen Amina of Hausaland in the 16th century and a record of dynasty of 17 Queens before her, yet there is an invisibility of Queen Amina in Muslim historical records. There is the Queen Hatshepsout of Egypt in the 15th century BC, the Queen of Sheba in Ethiopia in 1000 BC, and Queens titled Candaces of Nubia – some of whom fought the Romans. Of much relevance here is the fact that, according to Diop, there was no transition from matriarchy to patriarchy in ancient Egypt, because the social structure was essentially matriarchal –meaning female rule and female transmission of property and descent. Ancient Egyptian religion presents an example of a complementary gender ideological construction in gods and goddesses in the characterisation of Osiris and Isis. While as a god Osiris personifies corn, Isis as a goddess of fertility is a mother-goddess, characterised by influence and love, and like Osiris, she is goddess of corn, and inventor of the cultivation of corn, and is creator of all green things. Hathor was a mother goddess before these ones (Amadiume 1987). In these narratives, we have ideological, philosophical and cultural statements on environmental sustainability with a gender perspective from women voicing cultural standards.

When we look for women leaders of contemporary western-type states in Africa, we see women leadership in institutions continuing from precolonial Africa, such as women's dominance in the informal economy, for example, markets and market women's organisations and institutions, clubs, etc., such as market queens of the Igbo, Ashanti, Yoruba, etc. These market institutions are also the base of prominent women politicians, royal queens and princesses. We can see that women are cheated out of prominent top political positions in the inherited postcolonial state that has given us First Ladies. All of Africa is now independent from colonial rule, but out of the 54 contemporary African countries, there is only one woman elected president in Liberia, with lately another in Malawi as a result of political succession. The historical evidence of matriarchy in the social structure and women's leadership at the top are there, yet there is an absence of comparable presence of women at the top and favorable women-type institutions in the contemporary modern state.

South Africa

I have raised the question of culture and matriarchy in the context of the discourse on African endogeneity in research method and theory that best represent an African presence, and the historical experiences of the diverse groups of people in South Africa. Given the long history of apartheid in this region, a concern about the marginalisation of the San first people, not to mention other ethnic nationalities, is consistent with my focus on the importance of indigenous peoples and equitable gender justice for women.

Here again, a matriarchal perspective is a useful tool for countering the dominant patriarchal paradigm that ruled apartheid thought and practices, and it seems to be continuing in the post-apartheid state. It is in this context that I postulate a paradigmatic plurality in developing further the work on matriarchy, extending my idea of a matriarchal relational principle to other fields and disciplines for an alternative grand narrative of equity and social justice. This is a way of moving beyond colonialist interruptions and filling the empty spaces in our history and cultures. This method and theory bring an African perspective to the history and cultures of this region and particularly the history of the anti-apartheid struggle. It also restores balance in all aspects of the post-apartheid society and politics, giving prominence and justice to all its peoples, including restricted peoples on the Reserves, Bantustan, shanty-towns, refugee camps and deprived villages. A general critique of contemporary development concerns the unequal access to state resources, not just in terms of class, gender and race, but also by regions. This means that debate on the character of the contemporary state is still unresolved, even if purely judged from the perspective of a democratic and effective state for the delivery of services.

The Nile Valley

This brings me to the present excitement for democratic revolutions and transformations in the African Maghreb and North Africa, bringing a pan-Africanist perspective to some aspects of regional integration in view of the theme, 'Africa and the challenges of the 21st century'. With Egypt, Cheikh Anta Diop's classical domain of matriarchy and the present home of a world-renowned feminist Nawal El Saadawi, who titled her autobiography the daughter of the goddess Isis, I had read with excitement an article, in the spirit of the international women's day, at the height of revolutionary fervour the determination to include women in a meaningful way in the political process. What caught my attention was the view that the outcome in Egypt was going to set the women's rights agenda for the next decade.

Reminded of African women's historical and cultural achievements, some of which I have already mentioned, I was in anticipation of a great outcome, a revolutionary outcome, especially for women's rights, and marginalised indigenous peoples of this region. Since then, there has been a dampening of hope and dashing of great expectations, as recently articulated by prominent Egyptian women themselves, including Nawal El Saadawi herself.

My main point here is that from a historical perspective, short of equality, what politically is being offered women after modern revolutions and struggles is like crumbs off the table. Viewed in historical perspective, we see the contradiction. It was very disheartening to learn, in October, of a first woman ever that was running for president in Egypt's modern history in 2012! We had also read that her chances were 'slim to none'. The candidate, 49-year-old television presenter, Kamel, told IPS that she was running for president 'to show the world that Egypt is a modern country, in which women are afforded the right to vie for the highest positions of state, which – like the right to vote – is a basic human right'.

Despite Kamel's slim chances, Esmat al-Merghani, a political activist and Egypt's first female head of a political party (the Free Social Party), lauded her bravery: 'Buthaina's presidential bid will boost Egypt's image as a modern, civilised country,' al-Merghani told IPS. 'Even if she doesn't win, she will have opened a new door for the advancement of women – not to mention having had the honour of being the first Egyptian woman to vie for the presidency.' Kamel, for her part, was optimistic,

> 'When I talk to the people – even in bastions of tradition, like Upper Egypt and the Nile Delta – the fact that I'm a woman makes little difference', she said. 'What's important is that I hear their perspectives and understand their problems. I'm fully aware of the patriarchal nature of Egyptian society', Kamel added. 'But I believe I'm capable of leading the country's more than 80 million people; of leading a county of Egypt's longstanding political and cultural weight'. (see http://ipsnews.net/news.asp?idnews=105654 and the reproduced version in http://www.nationof change.org/first-woman-candidate-begins-campaign-1320077295)

To what do we attribute the shift of Egypt from matriarchy to patriarchy? From the perspective of gender and indigenous knowledge what can scholars make of the present demography of the Nile Delta in view of our interest in regional integration, and particularly the theme, 'Africa and the Challenges of the 21st Century?' A major point of Diop's gender-informed Afrocentric perspective concerns facing the negative historical and cultural claims and the effects of the colonial encounter and identity colonialism. It seems to me that in spite of a geographical and physical presence in Africa, the strong focus of North African feminists is a look north toward the orient, struggling within the discourse of Orientalism, and that is unfortunately informed by Eurocentric colonialism.

Contexts and Meeting Points

An indigenous gender perspective that takes into analytical consideration both local and international contexts and meeting points of African voices and perspectives gives Africa and African scholarship a better foundation and a progressive chance for self-determination and useful change. It also involves determining how to problematise difficult terms such as 'traditional' without losing analytical and theoretical advantage. African-Arab feminists self-identify as Arab without the African hyphen. (Eurocentrism and the implications of a colonialist map of Africa.) I again looked at historical maps of Africa. In the maps Morocco is African (see http://www.guardian.co.uk/global-development/interactive/2011/jul/11/a-political-history-of-africa-interactive)

In the 1900 map in this attached link, Morocco is African, unlike many parts of Africa that were wearing the colours of European colonisers.

In the 1914 map, only a small part of Morocco wears the colour of French colonisation, while most of the rest of Africa were colonised.

From 1914-1925, all of Morocco wears the colour of French colonisation, just as other countries of Africa are shaded under colours of colonisers.

During 1926-1940, it is the same for Morocco in spite of changes elsewhere in Africa, and the story still remains the same in 1940-50.

From 1951-1960, Morocco is again African, like most of the African countries which gained independence from European colonisers, except for the East and Southern African countries that were still under colonialism.

By 2011, all countries on the continent are African, and include a new one, South Sudan. All of Africa, as Africans, are well poised to deliberate on 'Africa and the challenges of the 21st century'.

Look at the personal statements of prominent Moroccan women, for example. Even though I can see African meeting points in their work, their orientation and self-identification is still Arab.

Laila Essaydi, an artist of 'Essaydi's art, which often combines Islamic calligraphy with representations of the female body, addresses the complex reality of Arab female identity from the unique perspective of personal experience.'

Her Personal Statement: 'By re-visiting and re-interrogating the Arab female body, I am tracing and mapping a history often coded in misunderstanding. Through my photographs, I hope to suggest the complexity of Arab female identity, as I have known it, and the tension between hierarchy and fluidity that are at the heart of Arab culture. But I do not intend my work to be simply a mere critique of either Arab or Western culture. I am going beyond simple critique to a more active, even subversive, engagement with cultural patterns to convey my own experience as an Arab woman' (http://www.kashyahildebrand.org/zurich/essaydi/essaydi002.htmlmale; http://www.kashyahildebrand.org/zurich/gallery/gallery093.html).

I have looked at some of her artworks. They are beautiful and you can see how she bends, emerges from and makes flexible the rigidity of Islamic patriarchal gender taboos in her imagination and her own image and body. But I do see a strong presence of African natural motifs and artefacts in her work, in spite of her self-identified Arab orientation.

Similarly, even though they self-identify as Arab, I have found meeting points with North African women sociologists whose works uncover pre-Islamic matriarchy through the study of pre-Islamic marriage and household gender relations, trade and commerce, property rights and ownership. Like Laila Essaydi, Moroccan sociologist Fatima Mernissi wages a struggle against the veil's restricting symbolism within the orientalist and not in an African discourse. Yet, there is much to gain from bringing her work south to look at the ways that African matriarchy domesticates and changes Islamic practices, gender and community relations in African Muslim societies, even in practices of the Sufism that Morocco shares with West Africa and the rest of Africa.

Just as I have argued for indigenous peoples, matriarchy and the useful importance of indigenous knowledge in Africa, indigenous peoples of the Nile Valley also provide sources of counter-hegemonic alternative possibilities to patriarchal dominance. A lot more literature is available on indigenous cultures of Africa south of the Sahara, but Diop's proposed regions for doing a sociology of history includes cultures of the Nile Valley and North African civilisations. There is the Andalusian civilisation that originated in Africa that impacted Spain, the study of which is well known in Europe and the Americas, but not brought into comparison in Africa. Recent events in North Africa are also exposing marginalised indigenous people whose study needs to be made known for comparative purposes.

Culture remains a unifying force where there is always a continuity in ritual, and where one can see the expression of shared rituals in the cultures of the indigenous peoples of the Nile Valley that echo themes in the cultures of the rest of Africa. People who do economic activities also do other things in their lives. The indigenous people, although marginalised, also constitute part of civil society with rights, in spite of disdain for the analytical terms that best describe their activities, especially as I have already pointed out terms such as 'traditional' and also 'rituals' and 'ceremonies'.

While bad and harmful aspects of rituals and ceremonies are outlawed and discarded, in spite of other dominant hegemonic presences that do harm to and disempower women, elements of life cycle rituals of indigenous precolonial cultures of African peoples, and, in some cases, continue into the present, yield a wealth of knowledge about African thoughts on gender identity and aesthetics.

This is particularly so in music, dance, food and art. Here I have in mind North African desert cultures whose practices also stretch down south of the

Sahara. I have always found fascinating seasonal and courtship rituals of pastoralist travellers, like the Wadaabe, the Berber, the Tuareg, the Peul and Fulani with related cultures. These people have institutionalized a beauty ideal through ritual in which both males and females consider themselves beautiful, and they come in all shades of colour. They practise role reversal in their ritual, celebrating love and beauty.

My point is that there is good and bad ritual, and we can move ahead with the good and useful things that women and indigenous people do to better our lives, bring hope, happiness, beauty and colour to a machine-oriented technology-dominated modern civilisation.

The strong campaign against female genital mutilation (FGM) and the presence of a large amount of literature on this subject makes it possible to propose and pursue with responsibility work on the pleasurable aspects of sexuality, the social and aesthetic self. We shouldn't confuse the medical negatives with the question of aesthetics and the erotic.

Sometimes, the debate has a racist superiority overtone both from abroad and from within, pointing to the class dimension that leads to a discrimination against indigenous African women by stereotyping them.

Leadership at the grassroots

On the all important bottom-up question of leadership at the grassroots, I have related a matriarchal theory to what I have described as saturated leadership with Igbo women's organisational activities in their communities. I find an African presence and comparative leadership expressions in experiences under Islam in the marginalised activities of women that some would describe as 'inarticulate powers' that are expressed through ritual symbolism.

Yet, there are different management, organisational, and communications skills that are very manifest in women leaders of healing rituals in all regions of Africa and the authority that they wield, not only among women, but also in their communities. The literature clearly shows race and class discrimination in marginalising these women, especially in Northern African Muslim societies. They are supposedly low class, slave descent, non-Arab Muslims. Race is a big issue for feminists of these regions to tackle in a feminist informed way.

Conclusion

There is a need to defend, uphold and affirm progressive and forward-looking gender perspectives and theories such as matriarchy and own the narrative as a major discourse. It is equally important to counter regressive perspectives and fundamentalist condemnation of assertive, women's ideas and personal choices that are often preachy, sermonising from particular offensive registers, ignoring or perhaps not even knowing much about the complex gender dynamism in African traditions. It is unfortunate that where African scholars hold back on the radical progressive ideas from African traditions, western scholars continue to appropriate and enrich scholarship and theory with our works and ideas.

We need a meeting of scholars, not politicians; but it seems that the politicians have gone ahead of the scholars in playing a leadership role in matters of African unity in the formation of OAU and the AU that replaced it. However, part of the discourse on history, culture, regional integration and Africa in the 21st century and beyond also includes more intense and honest examination of inter-regional relations in the past and their implications in the present, and measures for better relations in the future, particularly in matters of race, gender equity and social justice for all.

Reference

Amadiume, Ifi, 1987, *African Matriarchal Foundations: The Igbo Case*. London: Karnak House.

6

On the Postcolonial and the Universal?

Souleymane Bachir Diagne

'You speak as if the criticism of a particular conception of the universal were to be reduced to the contestation of the very idea of universality'. Seloua Luste Boulbina, 'An open letter to Pierre Nora', *Médiapart*, 10/17/11.

Léopold Sédar Senghor and his alter ego whom he called 'more-than-my-brother' (*mon plus-que-frère*), Aimé Césaire, devoted all their lives to this idea that to be genuinely, authentically, preoccupied with the question of the universal, is to make sure that all the different cultures, all the different faces of the human adventure harmoniously converge towards what the poet-president called, after philosopher Pierre Teilhard de Chardin, the 'civilisation of the universal'. This implies that no single civilisation should impose its 'universality', and that true *care for the universal* means *attention to the particular*.

Césaire wrote and published in 1956, a thunderous letter of resignation from the French communist party essentially because, among other reasons, its universalist conception of the liberation of all, depending essentially on the emancipation of the 'universal class' that is the proletariat, seemed to ignore the demand of those who had precisely been colonised in the name of the Universal. The question can now be posed: is the postcolonial anti universal? Shouldn't we say, rather, that only in a postcolonial world can the question of the universal truly be posed? This question is not just coming from the past. It has got a renewed topicality in France with what can be called the 'querelle du postcolonial', marked in particular by the publication of books such as Jean-Loup Amselle's *L'occident décroché* or Jean-François Bayart's pamphlet entitled *Les études postcoloniales, un carnival académique.* These books present themselves as a reaction to the arrival in France of 'postcolonial studies' in the wake of the 2005 riots in the suburbs of Paris. The reaction is to say that postcolonial studies, as the academic face of multiculturalism, is a 'machine de guerre' (Deleuze), a war machine against the universal, against science. So I want to address that very question here as a preface to a project of editing a special issue of the journal *Critique* on that topic. Let me formulate the question using the words of the Franco-Algerian philosopher, Seloua Luste-Boulbina, who, on 17 October, in the French online newspaper *Mediapart* (founded by Edwy Plenel a former Director of *Le Monde*) published a 'Lettre ouverte à Pierre Nora' in which she wrote: 'You speak as if the criticism of a particular conception of the universal were to be reduced to the contestation of the very idea of universality'.[1]

In my presentation I want precisely to show that the postcolonial world in which we live is an *ipso facto* 'criticism of a particular conception of the universal' but in the name of 'another idea of universality'. What Immanuel Wallerstein has called 'a more universal universalism', a truly collective, planetary universalism' (*European Universalism: The Rhetoric of Power* 2006). (This interestingly ends with Senghor's advocacy for 'civilisation of the universal').

On 7 May 1935, at the *kulturbund* of Vienna, Edmund Husserl gave an important lecture entitled, *Philosophy in the crisis of the European humanity*. The text of what is simply referred to as 'the Vienna lecture' was later revised and published as *Philosophy and the Crisis of the European Man.*[2] On that date, Adolf Hitler had been in power in Germany for two years and the process that would lead eventually to World War II was on the march. Because of those circumstances, Husserl's lecture took an air of 'a manifesto, in the true sense of the word' – to quote here the preface to the text written by Dr. Stephan Strasser – a manifesto for the European Idea, for a Europe which was thus summoned by the philosopher to recollect herself, to be herself again, to put herself back on her trajectory, or rather on the trajectory which she is, which is her unique identity, comparable to no other.

According to Husserl, that trajectory manifests itself as 'an extraordinary teleology, which is (…) innate only in our Europe' and which is 'most intimately connected with the eruption or the invasion of philosophy and of its ramifications, the sciences, in the ancient Greek spirit'.[3] Of course, Husserl explains, there is but one single humanity, which he describes as 'a single life of men and of peoples, bound together by spiritual relationships alone'. Such a precision is important: humanity is not the result of some zoological addition, as right-wing French author Alain de Benoist has written in his *Europe Tiers-Monde même combat.* Men and people seem to 'flow each into the other' as if they were the waves of a same ocean.

But it is also the case that when things are properly examined, humanity is seen to divide itself into plural humanities which present 'typical differences' that have nothing to do with the nation-states that were then witnessed to glorify murderous identities. Beyond such nation states, Husserl reminded the Europeans, there is the history and the destiny of the particular humanity that Europe is, particular because of a unique *telos* that erects her as a model after which the rest of humanity has every reason to conform itself while if she fully understands and does not forget who she is, she will find no reason to alter herself in some cultural contact. In Husserl's text it is as if the moving plea to Europe on the edge of self-destruction beseeching her to remember 'the inner affinity of spirit that permeates [all European nations] and transcends national differences', and to recapture the sense of 'a fraternal relationship that gives us the consciousness of being at home in this circle', would be more convincing if the feeling of its own excellence was stated in contrast and opposition to the others.

Thus, Husserl writes, taking as an example the imperial relationship that existed then between European (British) and Indian humanity: 'This [consciousness of being at home] becomes immediately evident as soon as, for example, we penetrate sympathetically into the historical process of India, with its many peoples and cultural forms. In this circle, there is, again, the unity of a family-like relationship, but one that is strange to us. On the other hand, Indians find us strangers and find only in each other their fellows. Still this essential distinction between fellowship and strangeness, which is relativised on many levels and is a basic category of all historicity, cannot suffice. Historical humanity does not always divide itself in the same way according to this category. We get a hint of that right in our own Europe. Therein lies something unique, which all other human groups, too, feel with regard to us, something that apart from all considerations of expediency, becomes a motivation for them – despite their determination to retain their spiritual autonomy – constantly to Europeanise themselves, whereas we, if we understand ourselves properly, will never, for example, Indianise ourselves'.[4]

I have quoted at length this passage because it is, I believe, the core of the 'Vienna lecture' and I will make the following remarks.

(i)   Husserl expresses a very peculiar aspect of the colonial project. What is in question is to 'europeanise' the rest of the world ('more or less', Husserl makes the precision, which means: inasmuch as it could participate in a 'telos' unique by essence) but this is not Jules Ferry's discourse: this is not the triumphant accent of the 'civilising mission', of a self-assured imperial project. The spiritual figure 'Europe' (for Husserl, America as well as the British dominions are part of 'Europe' while the Gypsies, endlessly wandering throughout geographical Europe, are not) is simply offered in its excellence as a model. As Emmanuel Levinas writes: to cultivate and to colonise are now separated. What was happening in Europe did not incite to triumphalism and, at the same time, the anti-colonial, anti-imperialist struggles of the 'non European humanity' were already announcing the end of colonial empires: the postcolonial was already in the horizon.

(ii)   My second remark concerns the possibility for the 'European Man' to understand what is not the European Man. Two different directions of thought are possible here. One is the affirmation of Europe's anthropological vocation which means that, from the vantage point of its own transparency to itself, it has the capacity to understand other humanities better than they can ever understand themselves. The other direction is the Levy-Bruhlian notion of a radically other 'mentality' that can never be penetrated by 'our' logic and our understanding. By using the categories of 'fellowship' and 'strangeness', Husserl adopts here the second direction.

(iii) The choice of India as an example is important. First, because India is the colony *par excellence*, being the jewel in the crown of the British Empire. Second because Husserl has in mind here that Indian philosophies are attractive for some European thinkers, Schopenhauer, for example, an attraction to which a sense of 'Indo-european' kinship is not foreign. But against such inclinations to 'indianise' as a consequence of 'studies on Indian, Chinese, and other philosophies' that convey the notion that other systems of thought could be considered 'different historical formulations of one and the same cultural idea',[5] Husserl insists that, even if the Greeks themselves evoked foreign influences on their own thought, the 'purely theoretical attitude' that defines the European *telos* is to be found nowhere else. If appropriation is a form of translation, it can only go from the universal to the particular or the subaltern (we know that the passage from the universal to the particular is called subalternation in logic). Statements that deserve to circulate only follow the direction from the universal to the subaltern. Therefore India, too, is 'strange to us'.

In sum, Husserl's view is that a world attached to the universal is a world in which it is essential that Europe should cease to give the impression that it has lost its *orientation* by compromising in forms of alteration (indianisation, for example) that could be compared to today's 'multiculturalism'. It is by remaining true to the direction set by its telos that it will play its role: the other humanities, sensitive to that 'something unique with regard to us' will feel naturally, 'apart from all considerations of expediency', as Husserl says, inclined to *orient* themselves after the European man.

Compared to that world oriented by and towards the universal, the postcolonial where Europe does not set the tone is, therefore, defined as *dis-oriented*. Thus Emmanuel Levinas, in *Humanisme de l'Autre Homme,* gives a picture of the postcolonial as '[a] saraband of innumerable and equivalent cultures, each of them finding its justification only within its own context', the consequence being for him: 'a world, that is admittedly *dis-occidentalised,* but also disoriented'.[6] From the colonial to the postcolonial one goes from a world where Europe finds in its anthropological vocation the justification for its capacity to understand the others better than they ever understood themselves and, therefore, to provide orientation for the rest of humanity, to a world in which 'provincialised' Europe is henceforth part of a 'saraband' where dis-occidentalisation is synonymous with disorientation.

The reason why Levinas' French word 'désoccidentalisation' has to be translated as 'dis-occidentalisation' rather than 'de-westernisation' is, of course, that the author's play on the opposition occident/orient in the French 'désoccidentaliser/désorienter' is to be kept. What is lost in such a passage is the universal, the very idea of a meaning that could be valid beyond one given context of cultural forms. And this is not simply a loss in translation: it expresses the very impossibility of translation, of a circulation of enunciations (*énoncés*) in a world that has been fragmented, where meaning has been *dis-located* precisely, because it is now recognised as always dependent on the *location* of its enunciation.

Is it inevitable that the discourse which presents itself as caring for the universal must construct itself as a denunciation of the multicultural and what it considers a substitution of the 'politically correct' to Levinas' demand that ethics be free of any 'cultural allusion or alluvium'?[7] Recent works devoted to 'postcolonial studies' in France, especially those by Jean-Francois Bayart and Jean-Loup Amselle, have answered 'Yes' to that question. Jean-Loup Amselle, in particular, interrogates the 'unhooking' from the West which is, according to him, the aim of postcolonial and subalternist studies. Thus the first lines of his *L'Occident décroché* [the West unhooked] repeat the theme of the equivalence between dis-occidentalisation and disorientation, when he speaks of 'a world upside down' witnessing a supposed 'crumbling of the West with the concomitant, competing raise of thoughts, of philosophies which dispute to Europe and America their intention to dominate the world, which means, according to those who have for them nothing but contempt, questioning their pretention to universality'.[8] For Amselle, if such a contestation has undeniably had a decolonising effect in the period that led to the independences, 'the prevailing situation in this beginning of twenty-first century is nevertheless very different from that of the 1950s and 1960s. In the present context of 'clash of civilisations', or rather, in what looks more and more like a crusades conflict, strategic essentialism has become a problematic notion as the affirmation of a radical otherness can be perceived as the ferment of all fundamentalisms. In the world we now live in, apparently open but in reality perfectly compartmentalised, we must abandon any definition or assertion of identity that restrains the circulation of enunciations through cultural boundaries, in other words makes those boundaries exist as such by reinforcing them. By leaning on some of the French Theory philosophers to give praise to the fragment, thus rejecting any overarching discourse, Spivak has exposed herself to being someone who ratifies a fragmented view of the world, which will only give ground to all sorts of fundamentalisms'.[9]

This passage can be read as the core of the book *L'Occident décroché*, in which Jean Loup Amselle criticises G.C. Spivak as an emblem of the postcolonial, in the name of a universal defined as the possibility for enunciations to cross-cultural boundaries without being swallowed up by the 'contexts' evoked by Levinas. It can be said that to translate the concept of 'strategic essentialism' as a 'praise of the fragment' misses the point that it is precisely a relational notion that does not exist but as a response, in the form of a resistance, pragmatic and ultimately evanescent, the way Sartre has written to propose the essentialism of Negritude that, like Eurydice, it is bound to disappear in a world where the other term of the relation is in the process of disappearing as well.

Anyway, Amselle contradicts himself as he both asserts that postcolonial discourse is an offspring of the anti-essentialism that characterises French Theory philosophies such as Foucault's, Derrida's or Deleuze's, and a manifestation of the fundamentalism and centrism of the fragment. *L'Occident décroché* presents the postcolonial as the image of a world in which what is called the 'Occident' (one should be here consistently anti-essentialist and not put on 'metaphysical lenses' as Said said in using that category as well) has secreted itself into the discourse questioning its own universality, and now finds itself, as a result, surrounded by what he calls the 'tricontinental thought' (an avatar of the centre/periphery distinction) which is but diverse ways of stating *centrisms* and *fundamentalisms*. Thus, I found myself presented in the book (in the excellent company of my friends, Gayatri Spivak, Mamadou Diouf, Mahmood Mamdani, Thandika Mkandawire, and others) as an 'orientalised afrocentrist', which is apparently a hybrid of African and Islamic centrisms.

If I allow myself to mention what is said about my work in *l'Occident décroché*, it is to insist on the way in which, in a very essentialist manner, Amselle characterised as anti universalist everybody who writes from ('from' is to be understood geographically and thematically) the space he constructed as that of the 'tricontinental thought'.[10]

I do think that the universal should be claimed. I do not think that the postcolony is a saraband or a world of separated provinces once Europe also has been provincialised, in the way the Copernican revolution had decentred our earth and projected it into space as a planet among the other planets. Like Amselle, in fact, I believe that enunciations should recognise cross-cultural boundaries and circulate, but that is simply to believe in *translation*. The demand for the circulation of enunciations is an empty one because what is not explained is which regime of enunciation? Where are the enunciations from? By who are they enunciated? etc.

Amselle evokes two aspects of the universal, one associated with the name of the Slovenian philosopher Slavoj Zizek; the second with the name of the Ghanaian philosopher Kwasi Wiredu. About Wiredu, Jean Loup Amselle reminds us of that author's firm belief in the existence of universals making intercultural communication always possible. Wiredu, he rightly says, insists on the translatability of all cultures and on the existence of common principles and values such as non-contradiction, induction, categorical imperative and morality.

These two examples to which he adds a reference to Rasheed Araeen and Dipesh Chakrabarty are meant to manifest the resilience, so to say, of universalism and 'the desire to preserve socio-political analysis against an exclusively populist or culturalist approach', even among the postcolonial thinkers that Araeen, Chakrabarty or Wiredu are considered to be.

The work of Zizek, which Amselle refers to, is a contribution to a volume with the very 'postcolonial' title of *Unpacking Europe* in which he presents what he calls a 'leftist plea' for universalism and Eurocentrism.[11] In his contribution, Zizek presents universalisation (rather than universalism) in opposition to globalisation, the latter having to do with the policing activities that global capitalism puts in place (organising market or conducting military interventions) while the former is the unsettling of the order thus established 'on account of the empty principle of universality, of the principle of equality of all men qua speaking beings, what Etienne Balibar calls *égaliberté*.[12] So Zizek can state that 'true universalists are not those who preach global tolerance of differences and all encompassing unity, but those who engage in a passionate fight for the assertion of the truth that engages them'.[13] The question to raise here is: one can certainly agree with Slavoj Zizek, and I do subscribe to the statement but why does it necessarily follow that a plea for universalisation should be the same as a plea for (leftist) Eurocentrism? His answer is that because the 'democratic politicisation' that is claiming *égaliberté is* uniquely European: 'the potential of democratic politicisation [is] the true European legacy from ancient Greece onwards'.[14]

Ultimately, the equivalence established by Zizek between universalism and Eurocentrism is simply the repetition of the same *telos* narrative. The simple fact that such a telos is now called *égaliberté* does not make the equivalence as such 'leftist'. Nehru already remarked in his *Discovery of India*, that he could not quite 'understand' the assumptions upon which Eurocentrism rests: (1) 'imagining that everything that [is] worthwhile has its origin in Greece and Rome'; (2) posing an 'organic connection between Hellenic civilisation and modern European and American civilisation' while it could well be said that 'the spirit and outlook of ancient Greece were much closer to those of ancient India and ancient China than of the nations of modern Europe'.[15] As Nehru writes: ' They all had the same broad, tolerant, pagan outlook, joy in life and in the surprising beauty and infinite variety of nature, love of art, and the wisdom that comes from the accumulated experience of an old race'.[16]

A leftist narrative of *telos* qua *universalism qua Eurocentrism* would simply mean that any demand for *égaliberté* from non-European humanity would still be, implicitly if not explicitly, in homage to a Europe that gives a meaning to it as the heir of the unique political configuration that made such a demand possible in world history. Now, after the tragedy of 17 October 1961, when a demonstration of

Algerians in Paris against the curfew imposed on Algerians only ended in a bloodshed by the police which was then under the command of Maurice Papon. The Algerian poet Kateb Yacine (1929-1989) wrote the following poem:

> People of France, you have seen everything
> Yes, seen it all with your own eyes
> You have seen our blood flow
> You have seen the police
> knock out the protesters
> And throw them into the Seine. The reddened Seine
> has not stopped on the following days
> vomiting in the face
> Of the people of the Commune
> those martyrized bodies
> Reminding Parisians
> their own revolutions
> Their own resistances.
> People of France, you have seen everything
> Yes, seen it all with your own eyes
> And now are you going to speak up?
> And now are you going to remain silent?[17]

The reference to the Commune of Paris and to a history of many French revolutions in the name of universal égaliberté is certainly not, in the words of Kateb Yacine, an acknowledgement of some French (or more generally European) unique *telos*. « leurs propres révolutions, leur propre résistance » is a reminder that elsewhere as well, resistance and revolution is also a 'propre', that the 'musulmans d'Algérie', as they were called, found within themselves, precisely within their being 'musulmans d'Algérie', the reason to protest and then found through Kateb Yacine' s pen that in so doing they were reenacting, translating something universal such as the resistance of the *communards*, the people of the Commune . As Senghor put it: 'each "exotic civilisation" has also thought of itself in terms of universality'.[18]

It all comes down to translation and the translatability that Kwasi Wiredu talks about. There is no universal language of enunciation. Paraphrasing Umberto Eco who famously said that the language of Europe is translation, it could be said more globally that the language of the universal is translation. To acknowledge that is to abandon the assumption that the exploration of a supposed universal grammar of the Logos needs to be conducted in the silence of the empirical languages that humans actually speak, while some of them, the European ones, especially ancient Greek and German according to Heidegger, can appear as its realisation, in some respect. Maurice Merleau-Ponty is one of the first philosophers to have articulated this notion of translation as the task of caring, in a postcolonial world, for the universal. He insisted on the importance of a tiny piece by Husserl insisting that it be included in the collection of his works. That piece is a simple letter that Husserl wrote to Lucien Levy-Bruhl, dated 11 March 1935, as a reaction to his reading of the ethnologist's *Primitive Mythology* published that same year. What makes that letter so important, according to Merleau-Ponty, is that Husserl admits in it that the philosopher could not have immediate access to the universal by reflection only, that he could not do without the ethnological experience of the diverse or construct the meaning of other experiences and cultures by simply varying, in the imaginary, his own experiences.[19] In a word, there is not an already constituted universality, with the stability of a *telos* overlooking, from its own self-assured exemplarity, anthropological proliferation and fluctuation (Levinas' saraband of innumerable cultures), 1935: same year as the Vienna lecture.

Merleau-Ponty has formulated for the postcolonial world the task of caring for a universal of translation: the universal is not any more the prerogative of a language, it is to be experimented and maybe 'acquired' through the lateral process of *translation*. The postcolonial universal, the non-imperial universal is precisely that: lateral. Merleau-Ponty establishes an important distinction between the two figures of universality in the following terms: 'the equipment of our social being can be dismantled and reconstructed by the voyage, as we are able to learn to speak other languages. This provides *a second way to the universal*: no longer the *overarching universal* of a strictly objective method, but a sort of *lateral universal* which we acquire through ethnological experience and its incessant testing of the self through the other person and the other person through the self. It is a question of constructing a general system of reference in which the point of view of the native, the point of view of the civilised man, and the mistaken views each has of the other can all find a place – that is of constituting a more comprehensive experience which becomes in principle accessible to men of a different time and country' (Merleau-Ponty 1964, 119-20).

It is important, and this will be my final remark, to note that if lateral universal is to be considered as translation, that does not mean transparency and identification. On the contrary, this is incessant testing. Merleau-Ponty, says the co-presence of many different views, in addition to the 'mistaken views about each other', are clear indications that the task cannot be to aim at a universal grammar or an operation of reduction to the same. The open-ended process of translation that lateral universal requires, because my point of departure is the language that I speak which is one among many, demands that we avoid both fragmentation and reduction to the One. That way of caring about the universal in a world liberated from the assumption of a universal grammar and the narrative of a unique *telos* is the Chaos-monde we have to deal with to end with a concept of Edouard Glissant.

Notes

1. « *Vous faites comme si la critique d'une conception particulière de l'universel se réduisait à la contestation de l'idée même d'universalité* ». Seloua Luste Boulbina, « Lettre ouverte à Pierre Nora », *Médiapart*, 10/17/11.

2. Husserl, *Philosophy and the Crisis of European Man* http://www.users.cloud9.net/~bradmcc/husserl_philcris.html

3. Ibid, p. 4.

4. Husserl, *Philosophy and the Crisis of European Man*. Available at http://www.users.cloud9.net/~bradmcc/husserl_philcris.html p. 5.

5. Husserl, *op. cit.* p. 8.

6. E. Levinas, *Humanisme de l'autre homme*, Fata Morgana, 1972, p. 55-56.

7. *Idem.*

8. Jean-Loup Amselle, *L'Occident décroché. Enquête sur les postcolonialismes*, Paris, Stock, 2008, p. 7.

9. *Ibid.* p. 146-147.

10. What Amselle calls ' pensée tricontinentale' is the addition and convergence of African thought coming from Africa especially Codesria, subaltern studies associated with India, dependence theory associated with Latin America (he also evokes the dimension of what he calls amerindianocentrism p. 191). He thinks that the American University plays an important role as the *locus* of 'tricontinental thought', suggesting even that in some respect it is the re-localisation of certain francophone African academics (say Mamadou Diouf or myself) within the American university that compels them to fully embrace a postcolonial perspective.

11. Slavoj Zizek, 'A Leftist Plea for Eurocentrism' in Salah Hassan and Iftikhar Dadi (eds.), *Unpacking Europe. Towards a Critical Reading*, Rotterdam, Museum Boijmans Van Beuningen, 2001; pp. 112-130.

12. *Op. cit.* p. 112.

13. *Ibidem* p. 122.

14. *Ibidem* p. 129.

15. See 'The Moment of Arrival : Nehru and the Passive Revolution', in *Nationalist Thought and the Colonial World*; p. 134.

16. Quoted in 'The Moment of Arrival...', p. 134.

17. *Peuple français, tu as tout vu*
    Oui, tout vu de tes propres yeux.
    Tu as vu notre sang couler
    Tu as vu la police
    Assommer les manifestants
    Et les jeter dans la seine. La Seine rougissante
    N'a pas cessé les jours suivants
    De vomir à la face
    Du peuple de la Commune

Ces corps martyrisés
Qui rappelaient aux Parisiens
Leurs propres révolutions
Leur propre résistance.
Peuple français, tu as tout vu,
Oui, tout vu de tes propres yeux,
Et maintenant vas-tu parler ?
Et maintenant vas-tu te taire

18. *On African Socialism,* p. 68
19. Merleau-Ponty, 'Le philosophe et la sociologie' in *Signes* (1960).

References

Amselle, Jean-Loup, 2008, *L'occident décroché. Enquête sur les postcolonialismes,* Paris, Stock.

Bayart, Jean-François, 2010, *Les études postcoloniales, un carbnaval académique*, Paris, Karthala.

Chatterjee, Partha, 1993, *Nationalist Thought and the Colonial World: A Derivative Discourse*, University of Minnesota Press.

Hassan, Salah and Dadi, Iftikhar (eds.), 2001, *Unpacking Europe. Towards a Critical Reading*, Rotterdam, Museum Boijmans Van Beuningen.

Husserl, Edmund, 1935, *Philosophy and the Crisis of the European Man,* http://www.users.cloud9.net/~bradmcc/husserl_philcris.html

Levinas, Emmanuel, 1972, *Humanisme de l'autre homme*, Saint-Clément-de Rivière, Fata Morgana.

Merleau-Ponty, Maurice, 1964, *Signs*, Evanston, Northwestern University Press.

Senghor, Léopold Sédar, 1964, *On African Socialism*, New York, London: Praeger.

Printed in the United States
By Bookmasters